Osip Mandelshtam was born in
brought up in St Petersburg. He studied at Heidelberg and
the University of St Petersburg. The first volume of his poetry, *Kamen*
(*Stone*), appeared in 1913 and was followed by *Tristia* (1922) and *Poems*
(1928). His persecution by the Soviet authorities for his evident lack of
ideological conformism began in earnest in the 1930s, and in 1934 he
was arrested and eventually exiled to Voronezh. He was finally re-
arrested in 1938. He died in Eastern Siberia, on the way to a labour
camp.

James Greene was born in Berlin in 1938. He took a degree in French
and Russian at Oxford and studied psychology and English literature
at London University. His second collection of poems, *A Sad Paradise*,
was published in 1990. In 1985 he won first prize in the British Com-
parative Literature Association's translation competition for his versions
of Fernando Pessoa and in 1986 second prize in the *TLS*/Cheltenham
Festival of Literature poetry competition. Earlier versions of some of
the poems included in the present volume were published by Elek
(1977), Granada (1980) and Angel Books (1988) and read at the
National Theatre, the Mermaid, Riverside Studios, the Voice Box
(Festival Hall), both the Oxford and Cambridge Poetry Festivals and
on Radio 3. Three of his translations of Mandelshtam are included in
The Oxford Book of Verse in English Translation.

OSIP MANDELSHTAM

SELECTED POEMS

SELECTED AND TRANSLATED
BY JAMES GREENE

FOREWORDS BY NADEZHDA MANDELSHTAM
AND DONALD DAVIE

INTRODUCTION BY DONALD RAYFIELD

PENGUIN BOOKS

PENGUIN BOOKS

Published by the Penguin Group
Penguin Books Ltd, 27 Wrights Lane, London w8 5tz, England
Penguin Books USA Inc., 375 Hudson Street, New York, New York 10014, USA
Penguin Books Australia Ltd, Ringwood, Victoria, Australia
Penguin Books Canada Ltd, 10 Alcorn Avenue, Toronto, Ontario, Canada m4v 3b2
Penguin Books (NZ) Ltd, 182–190 Wairau Road, Auckland 10, New Zealand

Penguin Books Ltd, Registered Offices: Harmondsworth, Middlesex, England

This selection first published in Great Britain, under the title *The Eyesight of Wasps*,
by Angel Books, London 1989
Revised edition first published under the present title by Penguin Books 1991

3 5 7 9 10 8 6 4

Selection, translations, Preface and notes copyright © James Greene, 1989, 1991
Foreword by Nadezhda Mandelshtam copyright © Nadezhda Mandelshtam, 1976
Foreword by Donald Davie copyright © Donald Davie, 1977
Introduction copyright © Donald Rayfield, 1988
All rights reserved

The moral right of the translator has been asserted

Printed in England by Clays Ltd, St Ives plc
Set in Monophoto Garamond

Except in the United States of America, this book is sold subject
to the condition that it shall not, by way of trade or otherwise, be lent,
re-sold, hired out, or otherwise circulated without the publisher's
prior consent in any form of binding or cover other than that in
which it is published and without a similar condition including this
condition being imposed on the subsequent purchaser

To Ron Holmes, Maxwell Shorter
and Antony Wood

Fine fingers quiver;
A fragile body breathes:
A boat sliding across
Fathomless silent seas.

1909

Few live for the sake of eternity.
But if the passing moment makes you anxious
Your lot is terror and your house precarious!

1912

And alone, infinity, I read
Your primer:
Your wild leafless herbal –
Logarithm-table of prodigious roots.

1933

Like poppies, your eyebrows
Open up a dangerous path.
Why am I in love like a janissary
With this tiny volatile red –
The pitiful crescent of your lips?

1934

Angelic criminal, cheeky schoolboy,
Alongside the Gothic a villain:
He spat on the spider-like law –
Incomparable François Villon.

1937

Aortas fill with blood.
A murmur resounds through the ranks:
– I was born in '94,
I was born in '92 . . .
And, clutching the worn-out year of my birth,
Herded wholesale with the herd,
I whisper through anaemic lips:
I was born in the night of January the second and third
In the unreliable year
Of eighteen-ninety something or other,
And the centuries surround me with fire.

1937

Contents

FROM *STONE* (1913, 1916, 1923 AND 1928)

FROM *TRISTIA* (1922)

Foreword by Nadezhda Mandelshtam

I think that the most difficult task in the world is the translation of verses, particularly of a true poet, in whose verses there is no discrepancy between the form and the content (or meaning) – both of them always new and but a bit different (with no great disparity between them) – and where the ego of the poet is always strikingly felt. Marina Tsvetayeva said she could write as Mandelshtam did but that she didn't want to. She was a great poet but she was greatly mistaken. She could be influenced by Mayakovsky and Pasternak and remain Tsvetayeva because they were *innovators* and therefore easily aped. But Mandelshtam composed verses *in tradition*, which is far more difficult to imitate.

Mr Robert Lowell's translations are very free; Mr Paul Celan's into German also free. But both are a very far cry from the original text. As far as I know the translations of Mr Greene are the best I ever saw. I can't give my opinion about the Italian translations, as I don't know Italian as well as English, French and German. As for Elsa Triolet's, they are as naïve and vulgar as she was.

Mandelshtam said that the contents are squeezed from the form as water from a sponge.* If the sponge is dry, there would be no moisture at all. So, to render the content – which Mr Greene has succeeded in doing – is to give, in a way, the form or harmony, the harmony which *can't* be rendered in translation, the harmony which is quite simple and at the same time mysteriously complicated. Poetry is a mystery.

Nadezhda Mandelshtam, 1976

---

* See Translator's Preface, page xx, for discussion of Mandelshtam's statement in its original context.

Foreword by Donald Davie

Of Mandelshtam's *Octets*, Robert Chandler has said that 'the inform-ing energy of the poem stems from, is a part of, the universal impulse to form, which leads equally to the creation of a petal or a cupola, the pattern of a group of sailing-boats or a poem.' And Mr Chandler may be right. Yet as I worked at the *Octets** it seemed to me on the contrary that Mandelshtam was distinguishing one kind of form from another, and was celebrating only those forms that are 'bent in', arced, the form of a foetus or a cradle, specifically *not* the open-ended and discontinuous mere 'pattern' (rather than 'form') that a group of sailing-boats may fall into.

I stress this because I am inclined to see in it the clue to what is distinctive about this poet, and what is distinctively daunting about the challenge he presents to his translators. If I am right, Mandel-shtam's poems themselves yearn towards, and achieve, forms that are 'bent in', rounded, sounding a full bell-note. Moreover, be-cause what the poems say is at one with the forms they find for the saying, we see why it is that, as Clarence Brown tells us, for Mandelshtam 'cognition' is always 'recognition' – *re*-cognition, a return upon itself, a 'coming round again'.

And nothing else, so far as I can see, will enable us to reconcile Anna Akhmatova's firm declaration, 'He had no poetic forerunners,' with his widow's no less firm admonition: 'Mandelshtam . . . unlike *innovators* such as Mayakovsky and Pasternak . . . composed verses *in tradition*, which is far more difficult to imitate.' What sort of a poet can this be, who is 'traditional' and yet has 'no poetic forerunners'? We solve this riddle by saying that in his techniques Mandelshtam was indeed unprecedented, yet the techniques were made to serve a *form* – why not say, simply, a *beauty*? – that rejoiced in calling upon

* Donald Davie's version of Mandelshtam's long poem *The Octets* was published in *Agenda*, vol. 14, no. 2, 1976.

every precedent one might think of, from Homer to Ovid, to the builders of Santa Sophia, to Dante and Ariosto and Racine. For it is true, surely: the sort of form to which Mandelshtam vows himself alike in nature and in art, the form of the bent-in and the rounded-upon-itself, is the most ancient and constant of all European under-standings of the beautiful – it is what long ago recognized in the circle the image of perfection. This profoundly traditional strain and aspiration in Mandelshtam explains why the Russia of his lifetime is seldom imaged directly in his poetry, and why, when it is so imaged, the image is overshadowed by others from ancient Greece or from Italy; it explains why domes and cupolas and shells (whether whorled or scalloped) appear in his poetry so often; and it explains why the hackneyed figures of the sky as a dome and a vault, and of the sea as curved round the earth's curve, appear in that poetry so insistently and with such otherwise unexplained potency. If we were to call Mandelshtam 'classical', this is what we might mean, or what we ought to mean. And nothing is further from what may reasonably be seen as the characteristic endeavour of the Western European and American of this century, in all the arts – that is to say, the finding of beauty in the discontinuous and the asymmetrical, the open-ended and indeed the adventitious.

Just here arises the peculiarly extreme difficulty of translating Mandelshtam into English. Before James Greene's, the most read-able and accomplished translation we had was by W. S. Merwin, done in collaboration with Clarence Brown. But this was, necessarily and properly, an *American* translation; a translation, that's to say, into that one of the twentieth-century idioms which is, and has been ever since Walt Whitman, and even in such an untypical American as Pound, pre-eminently vowed to the open-ended and the discon-tinuous. Yet Mandelshtam is the most 'European' of all Russian poets since Pushkin. How could Merwin have succeeded? Yet he did – to the extent that he does indeed bring over, for a public that has not and cannot have any immediate access to the Mediterranean fountains of European consciousness, as much of Mandelshtam as can survive that oceanic passage. Here however was a chance for that one of the English-speaking idioms which *is* part of the

European consciousness: could the British idiom achieve what by its very nature the American could not? James Greene had his own difficulties; for current British idioms, in so far as they respect the integrity of the verse-line and the verse-stanza (and plainly that was what was involved), characteristically give *pattern* instead of *form*, or else – to put it another way – they preserve the arc of the poem's form only by 'filling in', by not having the content of the poem pressing up against the curve of its form with equal pressure at every point. (The opposite danger, which I have not escaped in my versions, is of packing the content against the verse-line so tightly that the verse is felt to be straining and, as it were, bursting at the seams.) James Greene was equal to the challenge. His measuring up to it is shown in the first place by his daring to do what every verse-translator must have guiltily felt he ought to do, but was afraid of doing – that's to say, by leaving untranslated those parts of poems for which he could find no equivalent in English verse that carried authority. His more positive virtues – particularly in finding English near-equivalents for the punning resemblances in sound which, for Mandelshtam as for Pasternak, function as structural principles, given the richly orchestrated nature of Russian – can be appreciated only by those who can check back against the Russian originals.

Here for the first time we have a faithful version, not of Mandelshtam, but of as much of Mandelshtam as this scrupulous translator is prepared to stand by – faithful as never before, because as never before there is no line of the Russian poems that is not made *poetry* in English. Previous British versions have been wooden; this one *rings* – it is bronze, properly Roman bronze.

Donald Davie, 1977
Stanford University, California

Translator's Preface

> [Mandelshtam] had no poetic forerunners – wouldn't that be something worth thinking about for his biography? In all of world poetry I know of no other such case. We know the sources of Pushkin and Blok, but who will tell us where that new, divine harmony, Mandelshtam's poetry, came from?
>
> Anna Akhmatova

> Translation it is that openeth the window, to let in the light; that breaketh the shell, that we may eat the kernel.
>
> *King James Bible*, 1611:
> 'The Translators to the Reader'

The question of how to translate – should translations, like wives and husbands, be 'faithful' or 'free'? – has continued to be controversial ever since the literal-minded Gavin Douglas rebuked Caxton for his 'counterfeit' of Virgil, and Dryden (two hundred years later) aligned himself cautiously on the other side: 'something must be lost in all Transfusion, that is, in all Translation.' Where I sometimes add '*from*' to the number in brackets at the bottom of each poem, this is to indicate that, in these versions, lines (and sometimes whole stanzas) have been omitted, in an attempt to produce poems that work *in English*, as Pound's transformations of Rihaku do. Occasionally I compress two of Mandelshtam's poems into one. (Boris Bukhshtab wrote in 1929: 'in Mandelshtam's poetry every stanza is practically autonomous . . . Any stanza can be discarded or added.'* This was not intended by him as a criticism. I leave it to the reader to work out how or if this can be reconciled with Clarence Brown's statement concerning no. 39 that a poem for Mandelshtam

* *Russian Literature Triquarterly*, No. 1, 1971.

'is a structure of words that support and oppose each other, as a cathedral is a structure of stones that support each other'.)

Mandelshtam's poems are rhymed and strictly metrical, *Whoever finds a horseshoe* being the main exception. I have often had to eschew rhyme (but not half-rhyme, internal rhymes or assonance), and have tried to feel my way towards what might be the right rhythm for English.

To the non-Russian-speaking reader who wants to know about the relation between Mandelshtam's metres (which I have not consciously set out to re-enact), length of line, etc., and mine, I can only say: *total* 'faithfulness', were it possible – the 'same' metre, rhyme-scheme, pattern of sounds, number of syllables, line-length, etc., etc. – would be an absurdity; translations that attempt 'faithfulness' to metre and rhyme-scheme of the originals are usually *un*faithful in a more important sense: they fail to have the same *effect* on an English reader as the original on a reader in the original language.

In her Foreword Nadezhda Mandelshtam writes: 'Mandelshtam said that the contents are squeezed from the form as water from a sponge.' She is wrong. Here is a translation of what Mandelshtam in fact wrote in his essay 'Conversation about Dante':

> There is not just one form in Dante, but a multitude of forms. One is squeezed out of another . . . He himself says: *Io premerei di mio concetto il suco* (Inferno, XXXII, 4) – 'I would squeeze the juice out of my idea, out of my conception.' That is, he considered form something that is squeezed out, not as that which serves as a covering.
>
> In this way, strange as it may seem, form is squeezed out of the content-conception which, as it were, envelops the form . . .
>
> But only if a sponge or rag is wet can something be wrung from it . . . We will never squeeze any form out of it (the conception) unless the conception is already a form itself.

In connection with this, R. F. Holmes has written to me: 'I think Mandelshtam imagines the *concept* in the poet's mind being squeezed out by him in a *form* of words. Hence the *concept*, "strange as it may seem . . . *envelops* the *form*". If the mind contains no idea, the form-of-words coming out will be valueless; if the sponge is dry, nothing will come out of it.' Or, as Jennifer Baines has put it: 'Mandelshtam was tireless in his condemnation of those who advocated the separation of form from content.'*

Kiril Taranovsky, Nils Nilsson and Omry Ronen have in recent years addressed themselves to the question formulated by Akhmatova – 'who will tell us where that new, divine harmony, Mandelshtam's poetry, came from?' Thanks to their work (see Further Reading), we know much more about Mandelshtam's literary subtexts and contexts, and about the 'echoes and correspondences, reflections and refractions' which Henry Gifford alludes to in an essay on Mandelshtam and Dante,† and are better able to decipher the message of Mandelshtam's texts.

The Russian text I have mostly used, and the numbering of Mandelshtam's poems given in brackets at the bottom of each poem, come from his *Sobraniye sochineniy* (Collected Works), second edition revised and expanded, edited by G. P. Struve and B. A. Filippov, Inter-Language Literary Associates, Vol. I, Washington, 1967. But I have also referred to the latest texts. Rather more than fifty of the poems contained in the present selection were not among those translated by Clarence Brown and W. S. Merwin in *Osip Mandelshtam: Selected Poems* (Oxford University Press, 1973; Penguin, 1977).

The Soviet editions of 1973 and 1974, edited by N. I. Khardzhiev, are not as comprehensive as the American edition. Of the poems translated here the Soviet editions exclude (in addition to both Odes to Stalin, positive and negative) nos. 91, 165, 223, 233, 267/268, 307, 316, 318, 319, 320, 329, 341, 350, 351, 352, 353, 359, 368, 372, 380, 385 and 387, some for what must be ideological reasons.

In the following lines, written as a black joke in 1935, Mandelshtam indicated what his official fate would be:

> What street's this one?
> – 'This is Mandelshtam Street.
> His disposition wasn't "party-line"
> Or "sweet-as-a-flower".
> That's why this street –

* *Mandelshtam: The Later Poetry*, 1976.
† *Dante and the Modern Poet*, *PN Review* 12, Vol. 6, No. 4.

> Or, rather, sewer
> Or possibly slum –
> Has been named after
> Osip Mandelshtam.'

After Stalin's death Mandelshtam was 'rehabilitated', but there is still no street anywhere in the Soviet Union named after him.

Mandelshtam's Voronezh poems of 1937 appear in this book in a new order. This is the result of Jennifer Baines's authoritative commentary, *Mandelshtam: The Later Poetry* (1976). Her dating, which is based on Nadezhda Yakovlevna Mandelshtam's own typescript copy of Mandelshtam's poems, is definitive and supersedes that of Struve and Filippov's American edition (but the numbering of the poems printed here is still Struve and Filippov's).

Many of the 103 translations in this volume are based on earlier versions contained in a selection first published by Elek Books in 1977, reissued with additions and revisions by Granada Publishing in 1980 and then published by Angel Books under the title *The Eyesight of Wasps* in 1988. Since 1988 the versions have been revised again, often extensively, to keep pace with my understanding of Mandelshtam and to attain a more precise relationship with the originals; this has been achieved mainly with the help of R. F. Holmes's and Maxwell Shorter's superior knowledge of Russian.

Eight poems from the 1980 volume have been liquidated: nos. 66, 84, 235, 275–85, 346/347, 357, 362, 374. The following are added to the present selection: nos. 62, 109, 140, 164, 222, 223, 233, 258, 267/268, 286, a passage from *Journey to Armenia*, 296, 299, 306, 312, 316, 318, 319, 320, part of the Ode to Stalin, 360.

Some of the earlier versions first appeared in *Agenda*, *Bananas*, *Cyphers*, *English*, the *New Review*, *New Statesman*, the *New Yorker*, *Poetry and Audience*, *Quarto*, *The Times Literary Supplement* and *Willow Springs*; and some were used in Caspar Wrede's play about Mandelshtam, *Hope Against Hope*, put on in 1982 at the Royal Exchange Theatre, Manchester.

I want to thank R. F. Holmes, who with unstinting generosity has kept me at it over the years, and Donald Rayfield, who contributed the introduction and select bibliography. For this particular edition (1991) I am especially indebted to Katie Campbell, Robert Chandler, Stephen Duncan, Maria Enzensberger, Martha Kapos, Maxwell Shorter and Robert Stein, all of whom re-awakened my interest in these poems, brought them back to life for me; and to Richard McKane for invaluable information about the new and established textual variants (new since the Struve and Filippov edition).

James Greene, 1991

Osip Mandelshtam: an Introduction

Born in 1891, Mandelshtam came early enough into Russian litera-
ture to be formed by the cultural surge of the 1900s known as the
Silver Age. His father, an unprosperous leather merchant, was a
Latvian Jew whose written language was German; his mother, from
Vilno, was Russified in speech and outlook: 'Was she not the first
of her whole family,' wrote her son, 'to achieve pure and clear
Russian sounds?' Mandelshtam's first years were spent in Riga and
Warsaw. A decade earlier he might have become a Yiddish, German
or Polish poet, but in the 1900s discrimination in Russia was
breaking down and Jews who were Russian citizens began to feel
the Russian language to be their natural means of expression.

Jewish infancy was overlaid by a childhood spent in St Peters-
burg, and the education he received at the Tenishevsky school
(where Vladimir Nabokov was to study) helped to make him a
complete Hellene and European. His first lyrics show a passive
receptiveness to the Symbolist other-worldliness typical of the times:
Mandelshtam's receptiveness grew into a thirst for universal culture
once he had spent several terms listening to Henri Bergson at the
Sorbonne and studying at Heidelberg from 1907 to 1909. From
now on he was convinced that the poet's immortal creation far
outweighed in importance his mortal life: 'condensation vanish
without trace: The cherished pattern no one can efface.'

Mandelshtam's views on culture and the poet's vocation were
much influenced by the poet and poet's mentor Vyacheslav Ivanov
(1866–1949), whose dualities of Dionysian disorder and Apollonic
order became the energizing polarities in Mandelshtam's thought,
like the contrast of negative Judaic and positive Hellene, or Henri
Bergson's objective and subjective time. Equally important was
Mandelshtam's encounter with another great Symbolist, Innokenty
Annensky (1856–1909), headmaster of the Tsarkoye Selo lyceum
(the Eton of Russia). Annensky was a decadent poet of almost

pathological modesty, who likewise saw European and Russian culture as indissolubly linked to ancient Greece, a balancing act between orderly art and chaotic numinous forces. Annensky, as translator and disciple of Verlaine, Rimbaud and Euripides, inculcated a respect for language and poetic responsibility.

Meeting Annensky's pupil, Nikolay Gumilev, was even more crucial for Mandelshtam's future: Mandelshtam, Gumilev and the latter's wife, the charismatic poet Anna Akhmatova, formed the core of a new poetic grouping which formally declared itself in 1913 to be the Acmeists. The word and the ideology are in themselves insignificant: Acmeism was to be for the rest of these poets' lives 'a yearning for world culture', a sense of the priority of poetic tradition over individual lyrical ego, a reaction against the worst of Symbolism – its pursuit of the occult, of empty musicality, its cult of decadent autobiography. Although Gumilev was shot in 1921 and Akhmatova spent most of her life many hundreds of miles away, Mandelshtam always felt them to be addressees and collocutors.

Mandelshtam never renounced Symbolism: in *Silentium* he gave priority to the idea over the reality: 'Remain foam, Aphrodite,/And – word – return to music . . .' But his early poetry that was to be published in 1913 as *Stone* turns more and more to symmetry, affirming architectural principles not only as the criteria for lasting poetry, but as the means of surmounting the poet's own personal inadequacy. Notre Dame cathedral is seen to unite the negative and positive, Northern chaos and Mediterranean order in European culture, 'The Gothic soul's rational abyss,/Egyptian power and Christian shyness', and inspires him to declare: 'I too one day shall create/Beauty from cruel weight.'

The Acmeists, like the Bolshevik conspirators calling themselves 'hammer', 'steel' and 'stone' – Molotov, Stalin, Kamenev – stressed the positive with their 'hard' titles: Mandelshtam's 'Stone' matches Gumilev's 'Pearls', Akhmatova's 'Beads', Zenkevich's 'Porphyry', in tribute to Théophile Gautier's 'Émaux et Camées'. But their greatness lay in their 'softness', the vulnerable, tragic side that eventually breaks through. In Mandelshtam, the victim and exile are never utterly silenced: if not 'Joseph, sold into Egypt', then Ovid (exiled to the Black Sea steppes, like Pushkin and eventually Mandelshtam) is an ominous precursor. Ovid was to give Mandelshtam the title of his second book, *Tristia*, in 1922: but in 'Horses' hooves . . .' of 1914 the poet already acknowledges him as the poet who 'sang of the ox- and bullock-waggons/In the march of the barbarians'.

Unlike the other Acmeists, but like their French counterparts such as Paul Valéry and Jean Moréas, Mandelshtam had by 1912 become a Neo-classicist, reinterpreting the Mediterranean world as a timeless imaginary resource: the greatest poems of *Stone*, such as *The casino*, 'There are orioles . . .', 'Sleeplessness. Homer. Taut sails', merge the poet's mind with Homeric epic and Anacreontic idyll, so that the word becomes a world in itself: 'There are orioles in the woods, and length of vowels/Is the sole measure in accentual verse.' Time is bridged and the Hellenic world with its insecurity, an island surrounded by barbarians, undermined by Hades, is an analogue of the present: 'Now Homer falls silent,/And a black sea, thunderous orator,/Breaks on my pillow with a roar.'

By 1913, Mandelshtam was an original thinker as well as a mature poet. What is implicit in his poetics – the poet's ability to bridge time, to recreate past experiences in new languages – was made explicit in a daring series of intellectual forays. His essay on François Villon establishes a model for the poet as victim of the state; another essay, 'On the Addressee', makes imaginary conversation the basis of poetry; an essay on the first Russian thinker of note, the historiosopher Pyotr Chaadayev, argues the cyclic nature of history, for the need to interpret present experience as recognition of the past. These essays establish the role of the poet in history; they insist on continuity, on poetic language as a universal means of expression, constantly refined: they make Mandelshtam a proponent of Neo-classicism, which is to infuse and deepen his poetry for another twenty-five years, to an extent matched only in the work of T. S. Eliot.

The classical emphasis in Mandelshtam's *Stone* marked him apart from his fellow Acmeists: his lyrics have none of the egocentric, biographical core that we find in the best and worst of Gumilev and Akhmatova. Mandelshtam was even further in spirit and language from the Symbolists, whether the imprecise musicality of Blok or the occult rhetoric of Andrey Bely, while the dynamic barbarism of the Futurists, such as Khlebnikov and Mayakovsky, who were now denouncing European tradition in favour of experimental, aggressive poetics, could not have been more alien to him. Like Khodasevich, Mandelshtam had to wait for recognition simply because poets who were out to shock by self-dramatization or provocative manifestos drew more critical fire.

The outbreak of war brought unexpected roles to the Acmeists. Very few Russian poets, however, took refuge in patriotic self-immolation: Gumilev was virtually the only poet to expose himself to front-line bullets. The Acmeists were too heavily committed to a united European culture to feel anything but horror at the disintegration of centuries-old contours and unities. The omens of 1914 and 1915, the smouldering peat bogs around Petrograd (as St Petersburg became), the death of Russia's first challenger to Beethoven, Skryabin, seemed harbingers of an apocalypse; fire, the extinction of the sun and of genius. Rachel's shattering performance in Petrograd of Racine's *Phèdre* left a deep impression, as though not just a mythological queen, but a sun goddess and an entire culture were perishing. Premonitions turned Akhmatova into a Cassandra, made even the warrior Gumilev into a 'poète maudit' and gave the last poems of Mandelshtam's *Stone* an insight into historical necessity which made him from now on the most contemporary and, in the deepest sense, the most political poet in Russia.

Like Mayakovsky, Khlebnikov, Blok and almost every Russian poet liable for service, Mandelshtam got exemption from the army. His perambulations over Russia and its Black Sea territories began: a brief affair with Marina Tsvetayeva led him to the Crimea, the setting for much of his later poetry, Russia's only overlap with the ancient Hellenic world, and then to Moscow, which Mandelshtam, like Baratynsky a hundred years before him, could not help fearing as a threateningly medieval Asiatic world. The disasters of war and the outbreak of revolution, culminating in the irreversible October

1917, drove him not only to flight but to acts and words of desperate heroism: his protests to the head of the Cheka, Dzerzhinsky, against arbitrary terror, his willingness to collaborate in the highest sense, but not in the lower, with such amenable Bolsheviks as Lunacharsky and Bukharin, match the poems of his that greet the revolution as the 'twilight of freedom', 'the unbearable weight of power'. He not only mourns, but interprets and admonishes.

Mandelshtam begins to detect cycles in Russian poetry, too: the events of 1917 and 1918 lead him back to his precursors in the eighteenth century. Marina Tsvetayeva had acclaimed him as a 'young Derzhavin': he follows Derzhavin in his treatment of the dying Petrograd as a city about to pass into Elysium, 'transparent Petropolis,/Where Proserpina rules over us'. The poetry of *Tristia* aligns with the Petersburg themes of doom so powerfully stated in Pushkin's *Bronze Horseman* and in Dostoevsky's novels; only now Mandelshtam has allied them to imagery of the black sun that pervades French tradition, from the lines he attributes to Phèdre, 'With my black love I have sullied the sun', to Nerval's 'Soleil noir de la mélancolie'.

He was never again allowed by fate or the authorities to reestablish himself in Petrograd/Leningrad: for the rest of his life it remained what Rome was to Ovid, a dying homeland, the centre of a lost empire. Mandelshtam never proclaimed allegiance to a new proletariat order; he refused to redirect his poetry to the masses; his peregrinations during the revolution to the Crimea under the Whites or to Georgia under the Mensheviks were suspect; his loyalties to poets executed, like Gumilev, or exiled, like Vyacheslav Ivanov, condemned him to homelessness and eventually exile. In the eyes of the Soviet establishment he was a shadowy, even a shady figure: and the frequency of the word *ten'*, shade, shadow, in his poetry must be significant.

The Crimea, where Mandelshtam, like so many Russian writers, fled for warmth and food, became a fragile dreamworld. Here the White armies hung on until 1921 and it was possible to drink milk and honey, to relegate the reality of the north to the status of a recurrent nightmare. The title poem and the central poems of

Tristia oppose a carefully nurtured Hellenic dreamworld of sensuality to a threatening outside temporal force: these poems re-enact an opposition between internal time (in Russian, *vek*) and external time (*vremya*), very like the contrast we find in another assimilated Jew, Marcel Proust.

The sensuality of *Tristia* gives Mandelshtam's love poetry an almost palpable sonority: in 1919, he met Nadezhda Khazina; in 1921 he married her and a life-long dependence began, surviving his periodic infatuations which inspired some of the richest love poetry in the language. Like Catullus, whom Mandelshtam had studied very closely (despite failing his Latin examinations at university), he is moved by love when most threatened by death. The poem *Tristia* deals with the pain of separation from physical love, from life and from inspiration and from a culture as though they were all variants of one 'science of separations'. It is the culmination of the Russian elegy, which amounts to the major lyrical genre of the language, celebrating loss not merely of life but of love and language. Thus the first stanza's 'nocturnal laments when hair flows loose' are linked to the political betrayal implicit in the 'cock's clamour' of the second stanza and the poetic frustration – 'How threadbare the language of rejoicing!' – in the third stanza. After linking all three levels of experience – amatory, political and poetic – as firmly as Ovid ever had, Mandelshtam is able to draw the first of a number of statements on the separate role of men and women in tragic times. 'Wax is for women what bronze is for men,' he concludes, an idea which grows out of the different roles of himself as a victim and Akhmatova as a survivor, both Cassandra and Antigone, and amounts to a completely classical tragic philosophy. It holds true until the year before his death, when he addresses his young friend Natasha Shtempel with an almost unbearable summons: 'There are women who are natives of the sodden earth:/Their every step a hollow sobbing,/Their calling to accompany the risen'.

The Neo-classical craftsmanship of *Tristia* was greeted by sympathetic critics as 'the overcoming of Symbolism'; in fact, *Tristia*'s precision of tone is a preparation for the more starkly expressed revelations of the poetry of the 1930s. In 1922, however, Mandelshtam's achievement was more noticeable than a decade earlier: the Symbolists had died, emigrated or abandoned poetry; surviving Futurists, such as Mayakovsky, had lapsed for a while into versifying propaganda; the new proletarian poets were disappointing in their incompetence. Only Pasternak's *My Sister Life* – 'a cure for tuberculosis', as Mandelshtam generously acclaimed it – made a greater impact than *Tristia*, for Pasternak flooded his readers with sense impressions, private allusions and breathless inventiveness, quite unlike the orderly Hellenic imagery, the elegiac cadences and traditional sonorities of Mandelshtam. Before his execution, Gumilev had become disorientated enough to develop into a Symbolist; Akhmatova, on the verge of silence, had reduced poetry to austere aphorism: Mandelshtam was the only recognizable major Acmeist poet still writing.

Eventually, he made his way back from the Hellenic hinterland to Moscow, travelling over the Black Sea to Georgia three times between 1919 and 1922. Unlike Pasternak and Zabolotsky, however, he was never able to establish himself in the more hospitable Caucasus; too unsettled and outspoken to fit in with the ritual respect offered to poets, too preoccupied with the need to confront the moral vacuum at the centre of power, he returned to Petrograd and Moscow.

The proof that Mandelshtam was political is to be found in his heroic protests to Dzerzhinsky and Bukharin about Blyumkin, a secret policeman whom he caught filling in a blank signed death warrant with innocent names: this act put Mandelshtam's life at risk and may have contributed to his final doom. More important still are his much misinterpreted 'historiosophic' poems, such as *The Twilight of Freedom*, where the revolution is seen as a cosmic catastrophe, the earth out of its orbit, and the poet reacts with sympathy, not condemnation, for the leaders attempting to take the helm. Like Blok's *The Twelve*, such poems were misunderstood and condemned by left and right: the left could not forgive the elegiac tone and the right could not share the sense of tragic necessity. Those Bolsheviks, such as Lunacharsky and Bukharin, who could value such interpretations of their revolution, were few and very vulnerable. The real menace of the times was brought home to Mandelshtam in 1921 by the execution of Gumilev which, for all its self-willed martyrdom, was the first of several events that shifted Mandelshtam's allegiance to the world of the dead.

The world of the dead is ever-present in *Tristia*: Mandelshtam is constantly trying to retrieve his thoughts from the shadowy realm of Persephone, the refuge of Psyche, who symbolizes for him the free spirit, the unspoken word. 'The blind swallow flies back to her palace of shadows;/A nocturnal song is sung in a frenzy.' Swallows, the classical symbol of communication between the land of the living and the city of the dead, represent both free poetic thought and political freedom to Mandelshtam: the coming of totalitarianism he imagines as the 'binding of swallows into battle legions'. His poetics and his historical thinking are indivisible.

Mandelshtam's long-term view was perhaps even less acceptable to Soviet ideology than Gumilev's straightforward hostility. After *Tristia* Mandelshtam found his access to publishers more and more difficult. His attempts to settle in Leningrad foundered on hostility and he was forced by 1928 to settle in Moscow. The last poems of *Tristia* date from 1921: in any case the atmosphere for lyrical poetry was growing too rare. Russian literature felt itself to have reached an epic phase, where only narrative prose and the cinema could hope to assimilate what had happened. From 1922, Akhmatova and Pasternak virtually deserted lyricism for other fields, Akhmatova for the 'genre of silence', Pasternak for the illusive objectivity of narrative poetry, and Mandelshtam likewise moved towards prose as self-expression and translation as a means of earning a living. The Soviet reader naturally benefited from the influx of talent in translation and children's books, written by those who were refugees from their own thoughts, but the history of Russian poetry came to a decade or so's hiatus in 1923.

The 'other voice of prose' which Mandelshtam revealed in the mid-1920s was no mere surrogate, but an equally penetrating and perhaps even more original alternative to verse. The 'anti-memoirs' of *The Noise of Time* are a haunting evocation of the cultural influences – texts, teachers, childhood friends – on the adolescent poet, and the novella *The Egyptian Stamp* is a dense hallucinatory vision of the revolution and its effect on the naïve poetic persona. (Both works have been translated by Clarence Brown.) But this is more than autobiography, fictionalized or not: 'I want to speak about something other than myself, to follow the age, the noise and growth of time ... Revolution is itself life and death and cannot bear hearing people trivialising life and death. Its throat is dry with thirst but it will not accept a single drop of moisture from an outsider's hands.' But for all its importance as a vehicle for tracing his spiritual growth and measuring his distance and involvement, Mandelshtam, unlike Pasternak, never allowed prose to supplant verse. For a few years his poetry was undergoing a period of pupation before it burst out, metamorphosed and not immediately recognizable.

The relatively few poems of 1921 to 1924 lie halfway between the musicality of *Tristia* and the silence of the later 1920s: one's first reaction is to dismiss them as cryptic. But a reading of earlier Mandelshtam makes deciphering straightforward: the difference is that these are written for a familiar reader, who has mastered the code for his images' symbolic values. The density of 'I was washing at night in the courtyard,' which sets with minimal text a starlit night reflected in a rainwater butt, expands into sense when we remember the value of starlight as unalterable truth, salt as an image of painful realization, so that the eight-line poem becomes a cosmic contrast of eternal clarity and temporary murk, as stark and unmusical as a mathematical equation.

The compression of Mandelshtam's ideas of private and public time is most powerful in *My time* of 1923, where time is seen as a beast with a broken spine, turned cruel and vindictive, the poet unable to restore its unity. Here Mandelshtam has compressed an idea that goes back through Mayakovsky and Cubist painting to Verlaine, the idea of a whole human being as a musical instrument (the flute as the image of the spine, the vertebrae its keys), whose only purpose is harmony and which is destroyed when its integrity is broken: Verlaine's *Art poétique* and Mayakovsky's *Flute-Spine* are subsumed here, as is the classical tradition of Russian poetry,

Pushkin and Tyutchev, in the vision of nature still 'gushing out greenly' while human life is crushed to death.

Before his six years' silence, Mandelshtam also experimented with freer, more expansive forms, explicitly or implicitly odes, to deal with the vast disparities between an increasingly threatening Moscow and the starry eternity by which he had always measured events and time. Political imagery gives way to metaphors of predation, oppression and summary execution, traditional in Russian fable and urban folklore: *1 January 1924* has imagery of judicial murder: 'Lips sealed with tin', the Underwood typewriter with the cartilage of a pike and deadly 'layers of lime'. The imagery of threat and the astral symbols lie dormant until they surface with renewed effect in the 1930s. These six years, however unhappy in their wanderings and insecurity, were not entirely wasted. Like other Acmeists, Mandelshtam sought refuge in new spheres of activity, notably reading and translating Italian poetry, which seemed to hold the secret of survival in an age of lethal political conflict. Dante and Petrarch were soon to be of enormous significance to Mandelshtam as sources of themes, even new sounds, but above all as mapmakers of hell.

Hostility and suspicion in literary circles, even from such established pre-revolutionary figures as Andrey Bely, drove Mandelshtam into new intellectual regions. In the Soviet Union speculation was still relatively free among natural and physical scientists: the biologists and physicists so valuable to the Communists' development plans were the last reservoir of free thinking and international communication. It was among them that Mandelshtam found new acquaintance and ideas. Not until the 1930s were these new themes assimilated into Mandelshtam's poetics, but they were to give his poetry, and that of his younger contemporary Zabolotsky, resources almost unprecedented in European literature.

Even in *My time* of 1923, Mandelshtam shows an impressive familiarity with biological terminology; biology is the first of the sciences – followed by physics and cosmology – to enlarge his poetics. By 1930 he had made friends with Boris Kuzin, an eager proponent of neo-Lamarckism, a theory of evolution discredited before and since which propounds the inheritance of acquired characteristics and supposes that species evolve by an almost spiritual response to the demands of their environment. Stalin and his charlatan agronomist Lysenko favoured this pre-Darwinian theory for its implications in creating *Homo sovieticus* out of *Homo sapiens* and for the promise of training wheat to grow in the Arctic: very soon, however, the neo-Lamarckists were to be purged for the implicit idealism, even theism, of their doctrines. Mandelshtam went back to the original *Philosophie zoologique* of 1809 and saw something the biologists had ignored: Lamarck treats evolution as though it were literally a descent from warm-blooded humanity through the reptiles to the insensate protean forms of life and implies, as well he might after his bitter experience of the French revolution, that evolution is a reversible process, a ladder (*une échelle*) that nature could well descend or even snatch away. Furthermore, Lamarck's hierarchical survey of the genera and families of animals uncannily echoes Dante's nine circles of hell, each circle blacker and more painful.

Biology and Italian poetry are linked: the narrative thread spun by Ariosto in the poem of that name, the cult of the dead Laura in the Petrarch sonnets that Mandelshtam so lovingly translated in 1933, the yearning for an unattainable Florence and Tuscany in the poems of the 1930s all correspond to Lamarck's exploration of nature's abysses, the unattainable sixth sense in 'the lizard's pineal eye' (the fourth eight-line poem of 1934): these are secret worlds: as a variant of *Ariosto* puts it, 'Friend of Ariosto, Petrarch and Tasso –/ Senseless, salty-sweet language/And the charming bivalves of clinched sounds, –/I'm afraid to open the clam's pearl with a knife.' Their labyrinthine symmetry creates a structure that enables Mandelshtam to make tragic sense of Stalin's epoch.

This relevance of the Italian classics and of natural sciences to his predicament struck Mandelshtam on his last journey into Asia, a trip with biologists to Armenia that Bukharin's patronage had gained for him. The 1930s brought about the 'impact of Asia' on Mandelshtam and many of his contemporaries: for Russian poets, Armenia and Georgia had replaced Italy and France as lands where lemon trees bloomed. Given the traditional Russian associations of Asia with the blind tyranny of Medes and Persians as opposed to Europe's Hellenic freedom, it is only natural that Soviet poets should see ominous relevance in the cultural switch they were forced to make that accords with MacNeice's lines: 'For we are obsolete who like the lesser things,/Who play in corners with looking-glass and beads;/It is better we should go quickly, go into Asia . . .'

Dante, biology and Asia were the explosive: the detonator was provided by the second important death in Mandelshtam's career, that of Mayakovsky, which 'released the stream of poetry' in him, as his widow phrased it. If Mayakovsky, sympathizer and propagandist, could not live under the regime, then the 'genre of silence' appeared to offer no safeguards. However irrational the reasoning, both Pasternak and Mandelshtam experienced a 'second birth' on Mayakovsky's death: between 1930 and 1932 they wrote what are arguably their finest and boldest lyrics, using the last bubbles of freedom and the incomprehension of their censors to get them into print before twenty years of terror took poetry back to a purely oral genre.

In Tbilisi, on his way back from Armenia, in November 1930 Mandelshtam wrote a remarkable chain of stanzas to celebrate his reawakening to new, harsher textures, a 'cat language' of oral and written scratches and an Asiatic endurance of history's oppression. Years later, when Armenia has faded from his themes, the new sensations of being blinded and deafened by menacing colours and sounds are permanently incorporated into Mandelshtam's phonetic line and images. Armenia thus gives Mandelshtam not just a landscape for a new era – 'a costly clay' – but a new Asiatic language, rich in whispered consonants, fit for *sotto voce* and hermetic writing. But its history, the fall of a kingdom to imperial tyranny, is of allegorical importance in the prose account Mandelshtam wrote of his Journey. This poetic prose mingles history, landscape and travelogue with an account of Mandelshtam's induction into science, 'Around the Naturalists', and eventually gives rise to poems such as *Lamarck* of 1932 in which he identifies with the neglected 'patriarch' of evolution and prepares to experience his descent into the world of the arachnids, a typically spidery hell for Russian writers.

Between 1932 and his first arrest in 1934 Mandelshtam treats Russian, Italian and German poets in the same way as he does Lamarck, as precursors whom he must follow to the bitter end, whether the deviously self-sustaining narration of Ariosto or the arrogance of Pushkin's predecessor, Batyushkov, who pursued his 'eternal dreams, samples of blood,/From one glass to another' at the cost of his own sanity. Alien tongues are not just sources of new ideas, material for translation but – as Latin and Greek had been in the 1920s and 1920s – means for personal survival. Addressing the heroic *Sturm und Drang* poets in *To the German language*, Mandelshtam declares that 'An alien language will be a foetal membrane for me,/And long before I dared be born.'

Literary survival, however, was harder: the editor who published the *Journey to Armenia* was lucky to lose merely his job. Mandelshtam had enormous difficulty finding the meanest housing, was provoked by attacks and accusations into leaving the newly formed Union of Writers and was barred from publication. Then with suicidal spirit he composed a lampoon on Stalin – a talent for satirical verse had made him a successful children's versifier – and no one could save him. Stalin, who had himself been a Romantic poet in Georgia as an adolescent, took a close and deadly interest in Russian poetry: he would have been unlikely to forgive Mandelshtam's allusiveness, and the lines on 'His fat fingers slimy as worms', for all the acknowledgement of his power ('He forges his decrees like horseshoes'), were an eventual death warrant.

The intervention of Pasternak and Bukharin reprieved Mandelshtam. He was sent to a remote town in the Urals and after a suicide attempt was allowed to choose the steppe town of Voronezh for three years' exile. But his mental and physical health was broken and after the first wave of purges began in 1934 it was clear that this first arrest was only the prelude to a second and final blow.

For thirty years it was assumed that Mandelshtam had been destroyed as a poet: it was natural that, like almost everyone else, he should be silenced by fear if not by depression. Only after 1961, when his widow and the others who had stood by him – Akhmatova and Natasha Shtempel – released the manuscripts they had preserved in pillowcases and saucepans or reconstructed from memory and scraps of paper, did it become clear that there was a posthumous Mandelshtam, at first barely compatible with the known poet, to be disinterred from Voronezh. Slowly the poems have emerged in the Soviet Union, in *Literary Georgia* or *Questions of Linguistics*, and quickly they amassed in the West. Despite the loss of Mandelshtam's original manuscripts, the theft and destruction of much of his archive by self-appointed trustees or the NKVD, enough friends committed them to paper or memory for us to be sure that the versions now in print are as good as originals. (Many are variants, but as the notebooks were not fully prepared for publication we cannot always say whether one version of a poem supersedes another.) The Voronezh poems amount to a quarter of Mandelshtam's work and are arguably his finest. It has taken time for those who love the measured sonority of the early work to come to terms with the sometimes harsh, nervous and very dense language of the later work, and for the continuity between the two to become apparent.

What are now known as the Voronezh notebooks are 189 pages spanning three years: they represent three intense spurts spaced by long months of almost total silence: twenty-three poems date from spring and summer 1935; the second notebook's fifty poems come from nine weeks of the winter of 1936/7, while the last notebook holds about two dozen poems from spring 1937. The poems are precisely dated and show some thematic grouping: the first volume of Nadezhda Yakovlevna's memoirs, *Hope Against Hope*, should be read for the evidence of their authenticity and their origin.

The first notebook has to cope with a new landscape – the forests of the Urals and the black earth of the steppe so alien to Mandelshtam's urban or Hellenic scenery. Drawing on the phrase of Voronezh's famous nineteenth-century pseudo-folk poet Koltsov – 'step-mother steppe' (a pun in English, not in Russian) – Mandelshtam makes literal his own image of poetry as a plough digging up time, ('it ploughs the ear with a chilly, morning clarinet') and arrives at a surrogate of the musicality he needs in his surroundings: 'a mildewed flute'. That sense of a ruined instrument stays with his Voronezh poetry, culminating in the 'Greek flute' that slips from the poet's hands and lips in 1937. Far from the sea that moulded St Petersburg and the Crimea, Mandelshtam feels his new element, the black earth, to be fit only for the burial of 'This charred, bony flesh'.

A little work for radio in 1935, a sanatorium stay in Tambov, a visit by Anna Akhmatova, support from Pasternak and from Natasha Shtempel (who risked her own and her family's lives to befriend the Mandelshtams) enabled the poet, despite the new wave of purges sweeping the country, to gather his strength for the extraordinarily productive few months of the second and third Voronezh notebooks, in which all his interests, imagery and linguistic resources combined. Modern physics and Christianity he had already discovered to be linked in the work of Pavel Florensky, priest and mathematician, who proved that Dante's cosmology could only be reconciled with Einstein's theory of relativity: this stimulates Mandelshtam to new syntheses. Writing his *Conversation about Dante*, he treats himself as an explorer of hell, and he learns to face Christian demonology in the steppes. His lines, 'What can we do with the murderous plains?/. . . And is not he who makes us shriek in our sleep/Slowly crawling across them – /The space for Judases not yet born?', sound the same apocalyptic alarm as Yeats' 'rough beast . . . slouching towards Bethlehem to be born.'

Like every interpreter of the apocalypse, Mandelshtam begins to detect ominous parallels. His verse had always invested much of its power in rhyme, in the significance of assonance. In the poems of the second Voronezh notebook, coincidences of sound between opposites take on extraordinary meaning. The whispering 'cat language' – *k*, *p*, *t*, *ch* – of Armenian is combined with rich earthy sounds – *or*, *ar*; traditional Russian puns, such as the rhyme of *guby*, lips, with *gubit'*, to destroy, are enlarged. Words such as *os'*, axis, become crucial, since they link the poet (*Osip*) with his persecutor, *Josef* Stalin, and negative images such as wasps (*osy*). The weft is so elaborate that Mandelshtam now begins to defy translation.

A full understanding of this poetry is perhaps unattainable, even with the help of Nadezhda's memoirs, so varied and often private are the sources and references: Voronezh's art gallery, chance remarks by visitors as well as new reading merge with Mandelshtam's rekindled sense of his own Jewishness: 'I am plunged into a lion's den . . ./Under the leavening shower of these sounds:/. . . more potent than the Pentateuch.' Only in 1987, for instance, were Natasha Shtempel's memoirs published and the dedicatory import of many poems, such as 'With her delightful uneven way of walking', confirmed.

One clear development links the fate of the cosmos, the starry firmament, to that of the human skull, both vaults, repositories of truth now vulnerable to extinction. Poem after poem connects the movement of the human face, e.g. *The birth of a smile*, with the creation of order out of chaos, 'A rainbow ties them both together, A glimmer of Atlantis strikes both eyes', so that imagery of doom latent in the tender infant's cartilage and the lost city of Atlantis coexist with the affirmation of creation. Mandelshtam, at his serenest, achieves a Lamarckian acceptance that the 'escalator' of evolution has to go into reverse. Just as women's role is to mourn men, so the male poet's role is to mourn the universe: poetry remains for him what it always was – elegy. 'And I have accompanied the rapture of the universe/As muted organ pipes/Accompany a woman's voice.'

Serenity did not silence protest: by the end of February 1937, Mandelshtam's longest and most devious poem was finished: *Verses on the unknown soldier*. The title clearly destined it for publication: the naïve could read it as a lament for the victims of the First World War, as today the Soviet editors introduce it as a prophecy of the Second. It is only too obviously a lament for the still unsung victims of the purges, and ends with a cry of fear. But the most frightening aspect of the poem is its incorporation of modern quantum physics and astronomy (a subject on which Mandelshtam's namesake was then lecturing in Moscow University) and the anticipation of ideas yet to be born: the universe seen as a 'black oyster' in which starlight, once the source and image-bearer of ineradicable truths, is to be swallowed up. The starry vault whose image the human skull reflects is about to collapse. In this sense Stalin is a Copernicus capable of destroying cosmic harmony.

Mandelshtam redirected his attention to Stalin, forcing himself to the act of degradation inflicted on almost every poet, doomed or saved, in the 1930s: an ode to Stalin. But, incapable of simulation, he failed. Stalin appears as a counterpart to himself, the negative of the poet, sometimes through the same image, as an 'idol in a cave' surrounded by bones, trying 'to recollect his human guise'. Only in ambiguity could Mandelshtam attempt any conciliation. Like novelists such as Bulgakov and Zamyatin, he was interested in the mind and pathology of his enemy to the point of sympathy, but not of panegyric.

In April 1937, Mandelshtam was denounced as a Trotskyist: although his exile was coming to an end, he was living on borrowed time. That spring, inspired by the marriage of Natasha Shtempel as well as the suicides and disappearances in Voronezh, there is a final burst of lyricism, as though he were confident that the survival of his verse was assured. The influence of Keats (Nadezhda knew English poetry) seems to underlie his poems on the Cretan urns and the Greek flute, which stand for a continuous creative spirit that moves from one ephemeral vessel to another. The Greek flute commemorates not only a Voronezh musician who was purged, but the Hellenic creative spirit which the poet no longer has the strength to express: 'Clods of clay in the sea's hands ... My measure has become disease.' The Russian language seems to prove the involvement of death in creation: *mor*, disease, links with *mera*, measure, just as the syllable *ub* is present in the words for lips, murder, diminish. The Greek *thalassa* and *thanatos*, sea and death, are the beginnings and endings of poetry, as their assonance shows.

Mandelshtam was virtually the only important Russian poet writing in the mid 1930s. The purges had silenced every major talent. Pasternak wrote his *Artist* in 1936, during a brief lull in the terror, but soon succumbed to the prevailing atmosphere; Nikolay Zabolotsky relied on his Aesopic, fauve technique to write about the disjointing of the times, while appearing to praise the brave new world around him, but the censors understood him and he was swept away in the same wave that destroyed Mandelshtam. Even abroad, poetic inspiration had apparently deserted Marina Tsvetayeva: Mandelshtam had no cultural milieu, no critical response, no publications after 1934 and even his private readers were too frightened to respond. The Voronezh poems were written for the poet and a shadowy posterity: the lack of feedback is one of the reasons for their nervous, cryptic and compressed tone.

Their exile officially expired, the Mandelshtams managed to spend only three days in Leningrad and Moscow: they found temporary shelter in Kalinin. Then in spring 1938, with suspicious ease, they were found a place in a country sanatorium: on 2 May, Osip Mandelshtam was arrested. The protectors of poets at the court of Stalin were soon themselves to face the firing squad: Mandelshtam was processed as a counter-revolutionary and, starved, perhaps deranged, died in a transit camp in far-eastern Siberia on 27 December 1938.

With extraordinary determination, like the women at the cross, Nadezhda, Natasha Shtempel and Anna Akhmatova ensured his resurrection and the eventual triumphant entry of his poetry into the Judaic and Hellenic tradition. At enormous risk they preserved what they could in the chaos of the war years and the repressive years of Stalin's senility. A very few Russian critics, such as Khardzhiev and Shklovsky, and a few intrepid foreign scholars ensured that Mandelshtam's name, by the mid 1960s, became known not only to two new generations of Russian readers, but to virtually the entire world. As James Greene and, before him, Paul Celan have shown, Mandelshtam's concern for precision, musicality and continuity make him one of the most translatable poets Russia has ever produced. In Russian poetry, his influence began in the 1960s: as a protégé of Anna Akhmatova, Joseph Brodsky became a vector of Mandelshtamian poetics for Russian poets. While we cannot say that a tradition of Jewish verse exists in Russia, Judaism, as Mandelshtam puts it, 'like a drop of musk filling a whole house', adds a tension and internationalism to a lyrical tradition which could not otherwise have survived the rarefaction of the atmosphere.

Donald Rayfield, 1988

FROM

STONE

(1913, 1916, 1923 AND 1928)

The careful muffled sound
Of a fruit breaking loose from a tree
In the middle of the continual singing
Of deep forest silence . . .

(1)   1908

Suddenly, from the dimly lit hall
You slipped out in a light shawl;
The servants slept on,
We disturbed no one . . .

(3)   1908

To read only children's books, treasure
Only childish thoughts, throw
Grown-up things away
And rise from deep sorrows.

I'm tired to death of life,
I accept nothing it can give me,
But I love my poor earth
Because it's the only one I've seen.

In a far-off garden I swung
On a simple wooden swing,
And I remember dark tall firs
In a hazy fever.

(4)   1908

On pale-blue enamel,
Conceivable in April,
Birch-trees lifted branches
And eveninged imperceptibly.

Fine netting cut
Thin patterns exactly:
A design on a porcelain plate
Traced accurately

By the considerate artist
On his firmament of glass –
Knowing a short-lived strength,
Oblivious of sad death.

(6)   1909

What shall I do with the body I've been given,
So much at one with me, so much my own?

For the quiet happiness of breathing, being able
To be alive, tell me to whom I should be grateful?

I am gardener, flower too, and not alone
In the world's dungeon.

My warmth, my exhalation, one can already see
On the window-pane of eternity.

The pattern printed in my breathing here
Has not been seen before.

Let the moment's condensation vanish without trace:
The cherished pattern no one can efface.

(8)   1909

4

A sadness beyond words
Opened two huge eyes,
The vase of flowers woke up
And its crystal made a splash.

The whole room filled
With languor – that sweet medicine!
Such a small kingdom
To swallow so much sleep.

A little red wine,
A little sunlight in May,
And white delicate fingers
Break a thin sponge-cake.

(9)   1909

Words are unnecessary,
There being nothing to learn:
How sad and exemplary
Is an animal's dark heart!

It has no urge to instruct
And no use for words,
And swims like a young dolphin
Along the grey gulfs of the world.

(11)   1909

4-12-97

Silentium

She who has not yet been born
Is both word and music
And so the imperishable link
Between everything living.

The sea's chest breathes calmly,
But the mad day sparkles
And the foam's pale lilac
In its bowl of turbid blue.

May my lips attain
The primordial muteness,
Like a crystal-clear sound
Immaculate since birth!

Remain foam, Aphrodite,
And – word – return to music;
And, fused with life's core,
Heart be ashamed of heart!

(14)   1910

Ear-drums stretch their sensitive sail,
The widening gaze empties,
An unsinging choir of midnight birds
Swims across the silence.

I am as poor as nature,
As naked as the sky,
And my freedom is spectral
Like the voice of the midnight birds.

I see the unbreathing moon
And a sky whiter than a sheet;
Your strange and morbid world
I welcome, emptiness!

(15)   1910

Like the shadow of sudden clouds,
A visitor from the sea swoops down
And, nipping past, whispers
Along embarrassed shores.

An enormous sail austerely soars;
Dead-white, the wave shrinks back –
And once more will not dare
To touch the shore;

And the boat, rustling through the waves
As though through leaves . . .

(16)   1910

I grew, rustling like a reed,
Out of a dangerous swamp,
Breathing the air of a forbidden life
With rapture, languor, caresses.

In my cold and marshy refuge
No one notices me,
And I am welcomed by the whisper
Of short autumn minutes.

I enjoy this cruel injury
And in a life like a dream
Secretly am envious of everyone –
And secretly enamoured.

(17)   1910

Sultry dusk covers the couch,
It's stifling . . .
Dearest of all to me, perhaps,
The slender cross and secret path.

(19)   1910

How slowly the horses move,
How dark the light the lanterns throw!
Where they are taking me
These strangers surely know.

I am cold, I want to sleep.
Confident of their concern,
Suddenly towards starlight
I'm thrown at the turn.

The nodding of a fevered head,
The caring, icy hand of a stranger;
And, not yet visible to me,
Outlines of dark fir.

(20)   1911

Light sows a meagre beam
Coldly in the sodden forest.
I carry slowly in my heart
The grey bird, sadness.

What shall I do with the wounded bird?
The firmament is silent, dead.
From a belfry masked by mist
Someone has stolen the bells.

And the high ground stands,
Orphaned, dumb —
A white and empty tower
Of quietness and mist.

The morning, unfathomably tender,
Half real and half reverie;
Unquenched drowsiness;
The misty ringing of thoughts . . .

(21)   1911

a chorus of colossal bells in my chest

What you want never arrives
opportunely nor in reasonable measure.
Seize it. Vive de la vida lo sublime.

As poor as nature. I love that.
Minds. Hearts. Bodies. ¿Que mas hay?

The sea-shell

It may be, night, you do not need me;
Out of the world's abyss,
Like a shell without pearls,
I am cast on your shores.

Indifferently, you stir the waves
And immitigably sing;
But you shall love and cherish
This equivocal, unnecessary shell.

You shall lie down on the sand close by,
Apparelled in your raiment,
And bind to the shell
The colossal bell of the billows.

And your whispering spray shall fill,
With wind and rain and mist,
The walls of the brittle shell –
A heart where nobody dwells . . .

(26)   1911

taken up residence in my body, mi corazón.

I hate the light
Of the monotonous stars.
Salutations to you, my ancient delirium –
Altitude of an arrowed tower!

Be lace, stone,
Become a cobweb:
Lacerate the void
With a fine needle.

My turn shall also come:
I sense the spreading of a wing.
Yes – but where will the shaft
Of living thought fly?

My time and journey over,
Perhaps I shall return:
I couldn't love there;
Here – I'm afraid to . . .

(29)   1912

In the haze your image
Trembled; it troubled
And eluded me: mistakenly
I said, 'Good God!'

The name of the Lord – a large bird –
Flew from my breast.
In front: a swirl of mist.
Behind: the empty cage.

(30)   1912

No, not the moon, but a bright clock-face
Shines on me. Am I to blame
If the feeble stars strike me as milky?

And I loathe Batyushkov's conceit:
When asked the time,
His answer was – Eternity.

(31)   1912

The traveller

I am overcome by dread
In the face of mysterious heights;
I'm satisfied by a swallow in the sky
And I love the way a bell-tower soars!

I feel I am the age-old traveller
Who, on bending planks, above the abyss,
Listens to the snowball grow
And eternity strike on stone clocks.

If it could be! But I am not that wayfarer
Flickering against faded leaves:
True sadness sings in me.

There's an avalanche in the hills!
And all my self is in the bells,
Though music cannot save one from the abyss!

(32)   1912

The casino

I'm not in favour of premeditated happiness:
Sometimes nature is a grey blemish
And I'm sentenced, slightly tipsy,
To taste the colours of impoverishment.

The wind is playing with a tousled cloud,
The anchor scrapes the ocean bottom;
My mind, lifeless as linen,
Hangs over nothingness.

But I like the casino on the dunes:
The vast view from the misty window,
A thin ray of light on the crumpled tablecloth;

And, with greeny water all around,
When, like a rose, the wine is in its glass,
I like to follow the sea-gull's wings!

(33)   1912

The Lutheran

On a walk I came across a funeral
Near the Lutheran church, last Sunday.
An absentminded passer-by, I stopped to watch
The rigorous distress on the faces of the flock.

I couldn't make out what language they were speaking,
And nothing shone except fine brass
And reflections from the lazy horse-shoes
On the toneless Sunday side-roads.

In the resilient half-light of the carriage
Where sadness, the dissembler, lay entombed,
Wordless and tearless and chary of greetings
A buttonhole of autumn roses gleamed.

The foreigners stretched out in a black ribbon
And weeping ladies went on foot,
Red faces veiled; while, above them,
Nothing stopped the stubborn coachman.

Whoever you were, Lutheran deceased,
They buried you with ease and artlessness,
Eyes were dimmed with the decency of tears,
Bells rang out with dignified restraint.

I thought – no need for speeches:
We are not prophets nor precursors,
We do not delight in heaven nor live in fear of hell,
In dull noon we burn like candles.

(37)   1912

Hagia Sophia

Hagia Sophia – here the Lord commanded
That nations and tsars should halt!
Your dome, according to an eye-witness,
Hangs from heaven as though by a chain.

All centuries take their measure from Justinian:
Out of her shrine, in Ephesus, Diana allowed
One hundred and seven green marble pillars
To be pillaged for his alien gods.

How did your lavish builder feel
When – with lofty hand and soul –
He set the apses and the chapels,
Arranging them at east and west?

A splendid temple, bathing in the peace –
A festival of light from forty windows;
Under the dome, on pendentives, the four Archangels
Sail onwards, most beautiful of all.

And this sage and spherical building
Shall outlive centuries and nations,
And the resonant sobbing of the seraphim
Shall not warp the dark gilt surfaces.

(38) 1912

Notre Dame

Where a Roman judged a foreign people
A basilica stands and, first and joyful
Like Adam once, an arch plays with its own ribs:
Groined, muscular, never unnerved.

From outside, the bones betray the plan:
Here flying buttresses ensure
That cumbersome mass shan't crush the walls –
A vault bold as a battering-ram is idle.

Elemental labyrinth, unfathomable forest,
The Gothic soul's rational abyss,
Egyptian power and Christian shyness,
Oak together with reed – and perpendicular as tsar.

But the more attentively I studied,
Notre Dame, your monstrous ribs, your stronghold,
The more I thought: I too one day shall create
Beauty from cruel weight.

(39)   1912

Poisoned bread, satiated air,
Wounds impossible to bind.
Joseph, sold into Egypt, couldn't have pined
With a deeper despair!

Bedouin, under the starry sky,
Each on a horse,
Shut their eyes and improvise
Out of the troubles of the day gone by.

Images lie close at hand:
Someone traded a horse,
Somebody else lost his quiver in the sand.
The hazy happenings disperse.

And if truly sung,
Wholeheartedly, at last
Everything vanishes, nothing is left
But space, and stars, and singer.

(54)   1913

Horses' hooves . . . The clatter
Of crude and simple times.
And the yardmen, in their sheepskin coats,
Sleep on the wooden benches.

A clamour at the iron gates
Wakes the royally lazy doorman,
Whose wolfish yawning
Recalls the Scythians

When Ovid, with senile love,
Blended Rome and snow,
And sang of the ox- and bullock-waggons
In the march of the barbarians.

(60)   1914

There are orioles in the woods, and length of vowels
Is the sole measure in accentual verse.
But only once a year is nature lengthily protracted
And overflowing, as in Homer's measure.

This day yawns like a caesura:
Quiet since morning, and arduous duration;
Oxen at pasture, and a golden indolence
To extract from the reed one whole note's richness.

(62)   1914

Nature is Roman, and mirrored in Rome.
We see its forms of civic grandeur
In transparent air, like a sky-blue circus,
In the forum of fields, in the colonnades of trees.

Nature is Roman, and it seems
Pointless to trouble any gods again:
There are sacrificial entrails to foretell war,
Slaves to keep silence, stones to build!

(65)   1914

Sleeplessness. Homer. Taut sails.
I have counted half the catalogue of ships:
That caravan of cranes, that expansive host,
Which once rose above Hellas.

Like a wedge of cranes towards alien shores –
On the kings' heads godlike spray –
Where are you sailing? Without Helen
What could Troy mean to you, Achaean men?

Both the sea and Homer – all is moved by love.
To whom shall I listen? Now Homer falls silent,
And a black sea, thunderous orator,
Breaks on my pillow with a roar.

(78)   1915

Herds of horses gaily neigh or graze,
The valley rusts like Rome;
Time's translucent rapids wash away
A classical Spring's dry gold.

In Autumn as I tread the oak-leaves,
Thickly scattered on deserted paths,
I shall remember Caesar's lovely profile:
Effeminate features, treacherous hook-nose.

Now Capitol and Forum are far away,
Nature is quietly fading;
Even on the earth's rim I hear
The age of Augustus roll, a majestic orb.

When I am old may my sadness gleam.
I was born in Rome; it has come back to me;
Kind Autumn was my she-wolf
And August – month of the Caesars – smiled on me.

(80)   1915

UNPUBLISHED IN THE STRUVE/ FILIPPOV EDITIONS

Newly reaped ears
Lie in level rows;
Fingertips tremble, pressed against
Fingers fragile as themselves.

1909

TWO POEMS FIRST PUBLISHED BY STRUVE/FILIPPOV, 1964

The hunters have trapped you:
Stag, the forests shall mourn!

You can have my black coat, sun,
But preserve my living power!

(165)   1913

The old men of Euripides, an abject throng,
Shamble out like sheep.
I slither like a snake,
In my heart – dark injury.

But it will not be long
Before I shake off sadness,
Like a boy in the evening
Shaking sand from his sandals.

(178)   1914

FROM

TRISTIA

(1922)

– How the splendour of these veils and of this dress
Weighs me down in my disgrace!

    – In stony Troezen there shall be
    A notorious disaster,
    The royal stairs
    Shall redden with shame
    . . .
    . . .
    And a black sun rise
    For the amorous mother.

– Oh if it were hatred seething in my breast, –
But, you see, the confession burst from my own lips.

    – In broad daylight Phaedra burns
    With a black flame.
    In broad daylight
    A funeral taper smoulders.
    Hippolytus, beware of your mother:
    Phaedra – the night – stalks you
    In broad daylight.

– With my black love I have sullied the sun . . .
. . .

    – We are afraid, we do not dare
    To succour the imperial grief.
    Stung by Theseus, night fell on him.
    We shall bring the dead home with our burial chant;
    We shall cool the black sun
    Of its savage, insomniac passion.

(82)   *1916*

We shall die in transparent Petropolis,
Where Proserpina rules over us.
We drink the deadly air with every breath,
And every hour is the anniversary of our death.
Goddess of the sea, dread Athena,
Remove your mighty helmet of stone.
We shall die in transparent Petropolis:
Here Proserpina is tsar, not you.

(89)   1916

This night is irredeemable.
Where you are, it is still light.
At Jerusalem's gates
A black sun has risen.

The yellow sun is more terrible –
Hush-a-bye, baby.
Jews in the bright temple
Buried my mother.

Bereft of priests, devoid of grace,
Jews in the bright temple
Sang the service
Over this woman's ashes.

The voice of Israelites rang out
Over my mother.
I woke in a radiant cradle,
Lit by a black sun.

(91)   1916

Disbelieving the miracle of resurrection,
We wandered through the cemetery.
– You know, the earth everywhere
Reminds me of those hills

. . .

. . .

Where Russia stops abruptly
Above the black and deafly roaring sea.

From these monastic slopes
An ample field runs down.
As it was I didn't want to travel south
Away from spacious Vladimir,
But to stay there with that occluded nun
In the dark wooden village of god's fools
Would have spelled disaster.

I kiss your sunburnt elbow
And a wax-like patch of forehead –
Still white, I know,
Under a strand of dark-complexioned gold.
I kiss your wrist whose turquoise bracelet
Leaves a band of white:
Here, in Tauris, ardent summers
Work their wonders.

How quickly you went dark
And came to the Redeemer's meagre icon
And couldn't be torn away from kissing –
You who in Moscow had been so proud.
For us only a name remains,
A miraculous sound for a long time to come.
Take from me these grains of sand:
I'm pouring them from hand to hand.

(90)   1916

Out of the bottle the stream of golden honey poured so slowly
That she had time to murmur (she who had invited us):
Here, in sad Tauris, where fate has led us,
We shan't be bored. – She glanced over her shoulder.

Everywhere the rites of Bacchus, as if the world were only
Watchmen, dogs; you'll not meet anyone:
Like heavy barrels the peaceful days roll on;
Far-off voices in a hut – you neither understand them nor reply.

After tea we came into the great brown garden,
Dark blinds lowered like eyelids on the windows,
Past white columns to see the grapes
Where airy glass has sluiced the sleepy mountain.

The vine, I said, lives on like ancient battles –
Leafy-headed horsemen fight in flowery flourishes:
The science of Hellas in stony Tauris – and here are
The noble golden acres, the rusty furrows.

Well, in the white room silence stands like a spinning-wheel.
It smells of vinegar and paint and the cellar's new wine.
Do you remember, in the Grecian house, the wife dear to all
(Not Helen – another) – how long she spent weaving?

Golden fleece, where are you, golden fleece?
The whole journey a thundering of the sea's weighty waves.
And leaving his ship, canvas worn out on the seas,
Odysseus came back, filled with time and space.

(92)   1917

Spring's transparent-grey asphodels
Are still far away.
For a while yet sand rustles,
Waves seethe.
But here my spirit, like Persephone,
Enters the insubstantial circle,
And in the kingdom of the dead
Delightful sunburnt arms don't exist.

Why do we entrust to a boat
The weight of a funeral urn,
And celebrate the black rose festival
On amethyst-coloured water?
My spirit aspires there,
Beyond the misty headland of Meganom,
And a black sail shall come back from there
After the burial!

A shadowy column of storm-clouds
Quickly passes,
Under a wind-driven moon
Black rose-flakes scurry.
And memory's huge flag –
Bird of death and mourners –
Trails its black borders
Over the cypress stern.

And the sad fan of years gone by
Opens with a rustling sigh
Where the amulet was darkly buried
With a shudder in the sand.
My spirit aspires there,
Beyond the misty headland of Meganom,
And a black sail shall come back from there
After the burial!

(93)   1917

Tristia

I have studied the science of separations
From nocturnal laments when hair flows loose.
Oxen chew, waiting lengthens,
This last hour of vigil in the city.
And I honour the rituals of that cock-crowing night
When, having lifted the journey's burden of grief,
Tear-stained eyes gazed into the distance
And the singing of Muses blended with the weeping of women.

Who can know from the word *goodbye*
What kind of parting is in store for us,
What the cock's clamour promises
When a light burns in the acropolis,
And at the dawn of some sort of new life
When the lazy ox chews in his stall
Why the rooster, herald of new life,
Flaps his wings on the city walls?

And I like the way of weaving:
The shuttle runs, the spindle hums,
And – flying to meet us like swan's down –
Look, barefooted Delia!
Oh how meagre life's weft,
How threadbare the language of rejoicing!
Everything existed of old, everything happens again,
And only the moment of recognition is sweet.

So be it: a translucent shape
Like a squirrel's pelt
Lies on a clean clay dish
And a girl stares, bent over the wax.
Not for us to foretell the Grecian Erebus;
Wax is for women what bronze is for men.
On us our fate falls only in battles;
Their death is given in divination.

(104)   1918

30

Sisters: heaviness and tenderness bear the same insignia.
Wasps too suck the lungwort heavy as a rose.
Man dies, the hot sand cools.
Yesterday's sun is borne on a black litter.

Oh, heaviness of honeycombs, tenderness of nets:
It is easier to raise a rock than to say your name!
I am left with one care only, a golden one:
To free myself from the burden of time.

I drink the turbid air as if it were dark water.
Time is turned by the plough, and the rose was earth.
The heavy-tender roses, in their slow whirlpool,
Are plaited into double wreaths.

(108)   1920

Return to the incestuous lap,
Leah, from which you came:
Instead of Ilium's sun
You chose a yellow twilight.

Go, no one shall touch you.
On the father's breast, at dead of night,
Let the incestuous daughter
Bury her head.

But a fateful change
Must be fulfilled in you:
You shall be called Leah – not Helen –,
Not because imperial blood

Flows heavier in those veins
Than in your veins.
No, you shall fall in love with a Jew
And dissolve in him. God help you.

(109)   1920

When Psyche – life – descends among shades,
Pursuing Persephone through half-transparent leaves,
The blind swallow hurls itself at her feet
With Stygian affection and a green twig.

Phantoms quickly throng around their new companion,
They meet the fugitive with grievings,
In her face they wring weak hands,
Perplexed by bashful hope.

One holds out a mirror, another a phial of perfumes –
The soul likes trinkets, is after all feminine.
And dry complainings, like fine rain,
Sprinkle the leafless forest with transparent voices.

And uncertain what to do in this tender hubbub
The soul doesn't recognize the transparent trees.
Psyche breathes on the mirror, slow to hand over
The lozenge of copper to the master of the ferry.

(112)   1920

I have forgotten the word I wanted to say.
On severed wings, to play with the transparent ones,
The blind swallow flies back to her palace of shadows;
A nocturnal song is sung in a frenzy.

No birds are heard. No blossom on the immortelle.
The manes of the night horses are transparent.
An empty boat floats on an arid estuary
And, lost among grasshoppers, the word swoons.

The word slowly grows, like a tent or shrine,
Now throws itself down like demented Antigone,
Now like a dead swallow falls at one's feet,
With Stygian affection and a green twig.

Oh, to bring back the shyness of clairvoyant fingers,
Recognition's rounded happiness!
I am so afraid of the sobbing of the Muses,
Of mist, of bells, of brokenness.

They who are going to die can love and see,
Even sound can pour into their fingers,
But I have forgotten what I wanted to say
And a thought without flesh flies back to its palace of shadows.

The transparent one keeps on repeating the wrong thing:
Always *swallow, my love, Antigone* . . .
And on my lips the black ice burns,
The recollection of Stygian bells.

(113)   1920

34

4-18-92

For the sake of delight
Take from my hands some sun and some honey,
As Persephone's bees enjoined on us.

Not to be untied, the unmoored boat;
Not to be heard, fur-shod shadows;
Not to be silenced, life's thick terrors.

Now we have only kisses,
Like little furry bees,
Which perish when they fly from the hive.

They rustle in transparent thickets
In the dense night forest of Taigetos,
Nourished by time, by honeysuckle and mint.

For the sake of delight, then, take my uncouth present:
This simple necklace of dead dried bees
That turned honey into sun.

(116)   1920

*wreath
of dead bees*

Here is the pyx, like a golden sun,
For a splendid moment hanging in the air;
Now only the Greek tongue should resound,
Holding the whole world in its hands like an apple.

The exultant zenith of the service has come round,
Light under the dome inside the circular temple in July,
So that with nothing held back we sigh, beyond time,
For that green pasture where time stands still.

And the Eucharist hovers like an eternal midday –
All partake, play and sing;
Under the eyes of everyone the holy vessel pours
With inexhaustible rejoicing.

(117)   1920

Because I had to let go of your arms,
Because I betrayed your salty tender lips,
I must wait for dawn in the dense acropolis.
How I abhor these weeping ancient timbers!

Achaean men fit out the Horse in the dark,
They hack into the walls with their toothed saws,
Nothing can quiet the blood's dry murmur,
And you have no name, no sound, no copy.

How could I think you would come back, how could I dare?
Why did I break with you before it was time?
The gloom hasn't lightened and the cock hasn't crowed,
The hot axe hasn't yet split the wood.

The walls ooze resin like a transparent tear,
The town feels its wooden ribs,
But blood has rushed to the ladders and taken it by storm,
The men have been enticed three times in dreams.

Where is dear Troy? Where the imperial, where the maidenly
        house?
Priam's lofty starling-coop shall be a ruin.
And arrows fall like dry, wooden rain
And other arrows grow from the ground like hazel-nut trees.

The last star-pricks are dying out painlessly,
As morning, a grey swallow, raps at the window.
And lethargic day, like an ox waking in straw,
Stirs on the streets, tousled by long sleep.

(119)   1920

When the city moon looks out on the streets,
And slowly lights the impenetrable town,
And darkness swells, full of melancholy and bronze,
And songs of wax are smashed by the harshness of time;

And the cuckoo is weeping in its stone tower,
And the ashen woman descends to reap the dead world,
Quietly scattering huge spokes of shadow,
And strews yellowing straw across the floorboards . . .

(121)   1920

When, on my lips a singing name, I stepped
Into the ring of dancing shadows
Stamping on the tender meadow,
A mist of sound was left of what had melted.

To begin with I thought the name was 'seraph'
And I fought shy of such a light body,
A few days passed and I blended with it
And dissolved into that dear shadow.

And again from the apple-tree wild fruit falls,
And the secret form flickers in front of me,
Blaspheming and cursing itself
And swallowing jealousy's hot coals. ✓

Then happiness rolls by like a golden hoop
Fulfilling someone else's will,
And cutting the air with the palm of your hand
You chase the sweetness of Spring.

And it is so arranged that we do not dance away
From these spell-bound circles.
The expansive hills of virginal earth
Lie swaddled away.

(123)   1920

1-22-78

I like the grey silences under the arches:
Public prayer, funeral processions,
The affecting obligatory rites and requiems at Saint Isaac's.

I like the priest's unhurried step,
The winding-sheet's expansive bodying-forth,
Lent's Galilean gloom, like an ancient fishing-net,

And smoke of the Old Testament on glowing altars,
And the priest's orphaned cry. And royal meekness:
Unsullied snow on shoulders, wild purple vestments.

Hagia Sophia and Saint Peter's – everlasting barns of air and
        light,
Storehouses of universal goods,
Granaries of the New Testament.

Not to either of you is the spirit drawn in years of grave disaster:
Here, up the wide and sullen steps,
The wolves of tribulation slink; we'll never betray their tracks:

For the slave is free, having overcome fear,
And in cool granaries, in deep bins,
The grain of whole and perfect faith is stored.

(124)   1921

FROM

POEMS

(1928)

I was washing at night in the courtyard,
Harsh stars shone in the sky.
Starlight, like salt on an axe-head –
The rain-butt was brim-full and frozen.

The gates are locked,
And the earth in all conscience is bleak.
There's scarcely anything more basic and pure
Than truth's clean canvas.

A star melts, like salt, in the barrel
And the freezing water is blacker,
Death cleaner, misfortune saltier,
And the earth more truthful, more awful.

(126)   1921

To some, winter is arrack and a blue-eyed punch,
To some, a fragrant wine with cinnamon,
Some get their salty orders from the brutal stars
To carry back to smoke-filled huts.

A little still-warm chicken dung,
Sheep's muddle-headed warmth:
For life, I would give everything –
For so-much-needed care, for a match to warm me.

Look: in my hand there's only an earthenware bowl;
A chirping of stars is tickling my thin ear;
Through this pitiful down I have to admire
The yellowness of grass and the warmth of the soil.

Quietly to be carding wool and tedding straw;
To starve like an apple-tree in its winter binding;
Senselessly drawn by tenderness for everything alien;
Fumbling through emptiness, patiently waiting.

Let the conspirators, like sheep, speed over the snow.
Let the brittle snow-crust crack.
Winter – to some – is a lodging of wormwood and acrid smoke,
To some the stern salt of ceremonial wounds.

Oh to raise a lantern on a long stick,
Under the salt of stars to follow a dog,
And, rooster in pot, enter a fortune-teller's yard.
But white, white snow scalds my eyes till they smart.

(127)   1922

Rosy foam of fatigue on his sensual lips,
The bull furiously paws at the green breakers;
A ladies' man, no oarsman, he snorts,
His spine unused to its laborious burden.

An occasional dolphin leaps in an arc,
A sea-urchin comes into view. Hold in your arms,
Tender Europa, all his worldly possessions:
Where could a bull find a more desirable yoke?

Bitterly she heeds the mighty splashing:
The corpulent and fertile sea is seething.
Aghast at the water's oily brilliance,
She would like to slide down those hirsute cliffs.

Ah, she would prefer the company of sheep,
The creak of rowlocks or the lap of a spacious deck,
And fish flickering beyond a lofty poop. –
But the oarless oarsman swims with her further and further!

(128)   1922

44

As the leaven swells,
So the housewife's thrifty soul
Is possessed by the heat of the loaves,

As if Sophias of bread
Raise cupolas of rounded ardour
From a table of cherubim

And to coax a miraculous surplus
With force or caresses, the kingly herd-boy –
Time – seizes the bread, the word.

Even the stale stepson of the centuries
Finds his place – as the cooling makeweight
For loaves already lifted from the oven.

(130)   1922

I climbed into the tousled hayloft,
Breathed the hay-dust of the mouldering stars,
The dishevelment of space,

And on the ladder pondered: why
Wake up a swarm of sounds, the miracle of Aeolian order,
Athwart this everlasting squabble?

Once more I want to strike a match,
To shove the night with my shoulder –
To wake it up.

The huge and shaggy load sticks out above the universe,
The hayloft's ancient chaos
Begins to tickle as the darkness swells.

Mowers bring back
Goldfinches fallen from their nests.
I shall wring loose from these burning lines,

Get back to the order of sound where I belong,
To the blood's grass-like and ringing connection,
Nerving myself for the dream beyond reason.

(from 131 and 132)   1922

My time

My time, my brute, who will be able
To look you in the eyes
And glue together with his blood
The backbones of two centuries?
Blood, the builder, gushes
From the earth's throat.
Only parasites tremble
On the edge of the future . . .

To wrench our age out of prison
A flute is needed
To connect the sections
Of disarticulated days . . .

And buds shall swell again,
Shoots splash out greenly.
But your backbone is broken,
My beautiful, pitiful century.
With an idiot's harsh and feeble grin
You look behind:
A beast, once supple,
Ponders its paw-marks in the sand.

(from 135)   1923

Whoever finds a horseshoe

2 -13 -98

We look at a forest and say:
Here is a forest for ships and masts,
Red pines,
Free to their tops of their shaggy burden,
To creak in the storm
In the furious forestless air;
The plumbline fastened to the dancing deck
Will hold out under the wind's salt heel.
And the sea-wanderer,
In his unbridled thirst for space,
Dragging through damp ruts a geometer's needle,
Collates the rough surface of the seas
With the attraction of the earth's lap.

But breathing the smell
Of resinous tears oozing through planks,
Admiring the boards of bulkheads riveted
Not by the peaceful Bethlehem carpenter but by that other –
Father of journeys, friend of seafarers –
We say:
These too stood on the earth,
Awkward as a donkey's backbone,
Their crests forgetful of their roots,
On a celebrated mountain ridge;
And howled under the sweet cloud-burst,
Fruitlessly offering the sky their precious freight
For a pinch of salt.

Where shall we begin?
Everything pitches and splits,
The air quivers with comparisons,
No one word is better than another,
The earth hums with metaphors.
And light two-wheeled chariots,
Harnessed brightly to flocks of strenuous birds,
Explode,
Vying with the snorting favourites of the race-track.

47

Three times blest he who puts a name into song;
A song adorned with a name
Survives longer among the others,
Marked by a fillet
That frees it from forgetfulness and stupefying smells,
Whether proximity of man or the smell of a beast's pelt
Or simply a whiff of thyme rubbed between the palms.

The air dark like water, everything alive swims like fish,
Fins pushing aside the sphere
That's compact, resilient, hardly heated –
The crystal in which wheels move and horses shy,
The moist black-earth every night flung open anew
By pitchforks, tridents, hoes and ploughs.
The air is mixed as densely as the earth –
You can't get out, to get inside is arduous.

Rustling runs through the trees like a green ball-game;
Children play knucklebones with the vertebrae of dead animals.
The fragile calculation of the years of our era ends.
Let us be grateful for what we had:
I too made mistakes, lost my way, lost count.
The era rang like a golden sphere,
Cast, hollow, supported by no one.
Touched, it answered *yes* and *no*,
As a child will say:
I'll give you an apple, or: *I won't give you one*;
Its face an exact copy of the voice that pronounces these words.

The sound is still ringing although its source has ceased.
The horse foams in the dust.
But the acute curve of his neck
Preserves the memory of the race with outstretched legs
When there were not four
But as many as the stones on the road,
Renewed in four shifts
As blazing hooves pushed off from the ground.

So,
Whoever finds a horseshoe
Blows away the dust,
Rubs it with wool till it shines,
Then
Hangs it over the threshold
To rest,
So that it will no longer have to strike sparks from flint.
Human lips
        which have nothing more to say
Preserve the form of the last word said.
And the arm retains the sense of weight
Though the jug
        splashes half-empty
                on the way home.

What I am saying at this moment is not being said by me
But is dug from the ground like grains of petrified wheat.
Some
      on their coins depict a lion,
Others
     a head;
Various tablets of brass, of gold and bronze
Lie with equal honour in the earth.
The century, trying to bite through them, left its teeth-marks
     there.
Time pares me down like a coin,
And there is no longer enough of me for myself.

(136) 1923

1 January 1924

Whoever has been kissing time's tortured crown
Shall recall later, with filial tenderness,
How time lay down to sleep
In the snowdrift of wheat beyond the window.
Whoever lifted the sick eyelids of the age –
Two vast and sleepy eye-balls –
Hears everlastingly the roaring of the rivers
Of false and desolate times.

The potentate-era has orbs like sleepy apples
And a lovely earthenware mouth.
But it shall fall, expiring
On the overwhelmed arm of its ageing son.
I know life's exhalations weaken everyday:
A little more, and the simple songs of palpable injury
Will have been cut short,
Lips sealed with tin.

An earthenware life! A dying era!
What I dread is this: that you will be understood
Only by someone whose smile is helpless,
By someone who is lost.
What anguish – to search for a lost word,
To lift sick eyelids,
And with lime-corroded blood
Gather night grasses for an alien tribe.

What an era: layers of lime in the sick son's blood
Harden; Moscow sleeps, like a wooden box,
And there's nowhere to run to from the tyrant-epoch . . .
Snow, as of old, smells of apples.
I want to escape from my own threshold.
Where to? The street is dark
And conscience shows up ahead of me, white,
Like salt scattered for pavements

How could I ever betray to scandalmongers –
Again the frost smells of apples –
That marvellous pledge to the Fourth Estate
And vows solemn enough for tears?

Who else shall you kill? Who else extol?
What lie invent?
The Underwood's cartilage – quick, wrench out its key
And you'll find the little bone of a pike;
And, layers of lime thawing in the sick son's blood, ✔
Blissful laughter shall splash out . . .
But the typewriters' mere sonatina
Is only a shadow of former, mighty sonatas.

(from 140)   *1924*

her son
coming off
in Cult.
revolut.

51

TWO POEMS PUBLISHED IN

NOVY MIR,

(1931 AND 1932)

Armenia

11-25-97

(3)
Armenia, you call for colours –
And with his paw a lion
Seizes half a dozen crayons from a pencil-box.

Here the women pass,
Stark as children's drawings.
They bestow their splendour,
Their lionesque beauty,
And do not terrorize the blood. ✔

(4)
I've drooled over my dishevelled life, like a mullah over
      his Koran;
I've frozen time and haven't spilt hot blood . . .

(7)
Majesty of clamorous boulders –
Armenia! Armenia!
Summoning raucous hills to war –
Armenia! Armenia!

Unendingly journeying towards the silver trumpets of Asia –
Armenia! Armenia!
Lavishly scattering the Persian coins of the sun –
Armenia! Armenia!

(13)
Earthenware, azure . . . azure, clay . . .
What more is needed? Squint quickly,
Like a myopic shah, over a turquoise ring,
Over earth's mould, whose script and lexicon are ringing,
A festering text, a costly clay, ✔
By which we are tormented, stirred,
As by music and the word. ✔

(from parts 3, 4, 7 and 13 of 203–15)   1930

Batyushkov

Palaver of the waves . . .
Harmony of tears . . .
The bell of brotherhood . . .

Mumbling, you bring us
The grape flesh, poetry,
To refresh the palate.

Pour your eternal dreams, samples of blood,
From one glass to another.

(from *261*)   *1932*

POEMS PUBLISHED

POSTHUMOUSLY

Self-portrait

In the raised head, a hint of wing –
But the coat is flapping;
In the closed eyes, in the peace
Of the arms: energy's pure hiding-place.

Here is a creature that can fly and sing,
The word malleable and flaming,
And congenital awkwardness is overcome
By inborn rhythm!

(164)   1931

I was only in a childish way connected with the established order:
I was terrified of oysters and glanced distrustfully at guardsmen;
And not a grain of my soul owes anything to that world of
     power,
However much I was tortured trying to be someone else.

I never stood under the Egyptian portico of a bank
With ponderous importance, frowning, in a beaver-fur mitre,
And above the lemon-coloured Neva
No gypsy girl ever danced for me to the crackle of hundred-
     rouble notes.

Sensing future executions, from the howl of stormy events
I ran to the Black Sea nymphs,
And from the beauties of that time – from those tender European
     ladies –
How much confusion, strain and grief I embraced!

Why does this city still retain
Its ancient rights over my thoughts and feelings?
Fire and frost have made it more insolent:
Self-satisfied, doomed, frivolous, youthful!

Perhaps it's because I saw in a picture-book
Lady Godiva with her ginger mane hanging down
That I still secretly repeat to myself: Lady Godiva,
Goodbye . . . But I don't remember now . . .

(222)   Leningrad, 1931

Help me, O Lord, to get through this night:
I am afraid for her life, your handmaiden's. —
Living in Petersburg is like sleeping in a coffin.

(223)   1931

For the resounding glory of eras to come,
For their sublime stock of people,
I was deprived of the cup at the elders' feast
And my happiness and honour.

Our epoch's wolf-hound grips my back
Though my blood is not wolf's blood;
Squeeze me, rather, like a hat up the sleeve
Of the Siberian-steppe-fur-coat,

In case I see any trembling or mire
Or blood-splashed bones on the rack,
So for me blue polar foxes may shine
All night in their original beauty.

Take me into the night where the Yenisey flows
And the pine-tree reaches the stars,
Because my blood is not wolf's blood
And only an equal shall kill me.

(227)   1931

I drink to the blossoming epaulette, v· 4-97
To all I'm reproached for and won't forget:

Asthma and lordly fur-coat,
The bile of the Petersburg climate,

The singing pines of Savoy,
The jug of cream – Alpine joy,

And the oil paintings in Paris. I also rejoice
At roses in the Rolls-Royce,

Champs-Elysées benzine,
Proud English red-heads, quinine.

To the waves of Biscay! I drink, but what with I'm not sure:
The Pope's Châteauneuf, a happy Spumante, or . . .?

(233)   1932

Impressionism

The painter portrayed for us
Lilac's violent swoon
And laid on the canvas, like scabs,
Colour's sonorous gradations.

He knew the density of oil –
Its pastry summer
Baked with violet marrow,
Dilating in its oven.

Even more violet is that shadow there:
A whistling or whip dying like a match,
So that you'd say: chefs in the kitchen
Are preparing plump pigeons.

Veils merely sketched,
A swing you have to guess,
And in this disorder of dusk,
Already a bee keeps house.

(258) 1932

Ariosto

It's cold in Europe, Italy is dark,
And power barbarous like the hands of Peter the Great.
Oh to throw wide open, as soon as possible,
A vast window on the Adriatic.

And I delight in his frenzied leisure:
Babble of sweet and sour, lovely oyster-sounds —
The whirr of a hundred whips. With a knife
I shrink from exposing such a pearl.

Through his window he smiles at the butcher's stall:
The child, asleep under a net of blue flies;
The soldiers of the Duke now drunk
On wine and garlic and on plague.

Dear Ariosto, maybe a century shall pass —
And we shall pour your azure and our black together
Into one fraternal, vast, blue-black sea.
We were there too. We too drank mead.

(from 267 and 268)   1933, 1936

64

We exist, without sensing our country beneath us,
Ten steps away our words evaporate,

But where there are enough for half a conversation
We always commemorate the Kremlin's man of the mountains.

His fat fingers slimy as worms,
His words dependable as weights of measure.

His cockroach moustache chuckles,
His top-boots gleam.

And around him a riff-raff of scraggy-necked chiefs;
He plays with the lackeydoms of half-men

Who warble, or miaow, or whimper.
He alone prods and probes.

He forges decree after decree like horseshoes:
In the groin, brain, forehead, eye.

Whoever is being executed – there's raspberry compote
And the gigantic torso of the Georgian.

(286) 1933

Chen Pan
- needs to be more mixed
- quick to anger
- unsympathetic at times

1. The body of King Arshak is unwashed, his beard runs wild.
2. His fingernails are broken, and wood-lice crawl across his face.
3. His ears, grown dull with silence, once listened to Greek music.
4. His tongue is scabbed from jailer's food – which once pressed grapes against the palate and was adroit like the tip of a flautist's tongue.
5. The seed of Arshak has withered in his scrotum and his voice is sparse as the bleating of a sheep.
6. King Shapukh, thinks Arshak, has got the better of me and, worse, has taken my air for himself!
7. The Assyrian holds my heart in his hand.
8. He commands my hair and fingernails. He grows my beard and swallows my spit, so used has he become to the thought that I am to be found here – in the fortress of Aniush.
9. The Kushan people rose up against Shapukh.
10. They snapped the frontier at an undefended place like a silken thread.
11. Like an eyelash in his eye, the attack pricked King Shapukh.
12. Both enemies screwed up their eyes, so as not to see each other.
13. Darmastat, the most gracious and best-educated of the eunuchs, encouraged the commander of the cavalry from the centre of Shapukh's army. Darmastat wormed his way into favour, snatched his master, like a chess-piece, out of danger, remaining all the while in public view.
14. He had been governor of the province of Andekh in the days when Arshak's velvet voice gave orders.
15. Yesterday Arshak was a king, but today is fallen into a crevice, huddles like a baby in the womb, and warms himself with lice, enjoying the itch.
16. When the time came for his reward, Darmastat's request tickled the Assyrian's keen ears like a feather:
17. Give me a pass to the fortress of Aniush. I should like Arshak to spend one more day, full of sounds, taste and smell, as it used to be when he entertained himself at the chase and saw to the planting of trees.

(from 8, 'Alagez' of Journey to Armenia*)   1933*

Your narrow shoulders are to redden under scourges,
Redden under scourges and to burn in frosts.

Your child-like arms are to lift heavy irons,
To lift heavy irons and to sew mail-bags.

Your tender soles are to walk barefoot on glass,
Barefoot on glass and blood-stained sand.

And I am here to burn for you like a black candle,
Burn like a black candle and not dare to pray.

(296)   1934

Black earth

Over-esteemed, too-black, all in peak condition,
Everything groomed withers, everything aired;
Everything crumbling, coming together like a choir –
Wet clods of my 'soil and freedom'!

In the days of early ploughing – black, almost blue.
And this is the foundation of unwarlike work –
A thousand mounds of furrowed language:
And something unbounded within these bounds!

And yet the earth is – a blunder, a blunt axe-head;
One cannot implore the earth, even if one falls at its feet:
Still it whets the hearing like a mildewed flute;
It ploughs the ear with a chilly, morning clarinet.

How pleasing fatty topsoil is to ploughshare,
How silent the steppe in its April upheaval!
Well, I wish you well, black earth: be firm, sharp-eyed . . .
A black-voiced silence is at work.

(299)   April 1935

Yes, I'm lying in the earth, moving my lips,
But what I'm going to say every schoolboy shall know by
    heart:

The earth is at its roundest on Red Square
And its unchained curve is hard,

On Red Square the earth is at its roundest
And its curve, rolling all the way down to the rice fields,

Is unexpectedly expansive
While there are still any slaves on the earth.

(306). May 1935

You took away my seas and running jumps and sky
And propped my foot against the violent earth.
Where could this brilliant calculation get you?
You couldn't take away my muttering lips.

(307)   May 1935

My country conversed with me,
Spoiled me, scolded, didn't listen.
She only noticed me when,
Grown-up, I became an eye-witness.
Then suddenly, like a lens, she set me on fire
With a beam from the Admiralty spire.

(part 6 of 312)   May–June 1935

For those hundred-carat ingots, Roman nights,
Those breasts enticing the young Goethe,

Let me be answerable, but not lose all my rights.
There is a multifaceted life beyond the law.

(316)   June 1935

A wave advances – one wave breaking another's backbone,
Flinging itself at the moon in slavish yearning.
And a young janissary of a whirlpool –
In its untiring tidal metropolis –
Raves, slant-eyed, digging its ditch in the sand.

But through the flaky gloom
An unbuilt wall's pale teeth rise up.
The soldiers of suspicious sultans
Fall from foaming stairs – dismembered, spattered.
Cold eunuchs bring the poison in.

(319)   July 1935

I shall perform a smoky rite:
In this opal here, in my disgrace,
I see a seaside summer's strawberries –
Cleft cornelians
And their brothers, agates like ants.

But a pebble from the sea's depths,
A simple soldier,
Is more dear to me:
Grey, wild,
That no one wants.

(318)   July 1935

I shall not return my borrowed dust
To the earth,
Like a white floury butterfly.
I will this thinking body –
This charred, bony flesh,
Alive to its own span –
To turn into a street, a country.

(from 320) 21 July 1935

I can't make sense of today –
A day somehow yellow-mouthed.
Dock gates stare at me
From anchors and mist.

Through faded water a convoy of battleships
Moves quietly, quietly,
And the narrow pencil-box canals
Look even blacker under ice.

(329)   9–28 December 1936

Like a belated present,
Winter is now palpable:
I like its initial,
Diffident sweep.

Its terror is beautiful,
Like the beginning of dreadful deeds:
Even ravens are alarmed·
By the leafless circle.

But precariously more powerful than anything
Is its bulging blueness:
The half-formed ice on the river's brow,
Lullabying unsleepingly . . .

(336)   29–30 December 1936

I would sing of him who shifted the axis of the world . . .
See, Aeschylus, how I weep as I draw the portrait of
    the Leader . . .
In the friendship of his wise eyes
One suddenly sees – a father! . . .
(His *powerful* eyes – sternly kind . . .)
And I want to thank the hills
That nourished this gristle, this wrist.
He was born in the mountains and knew the bitterness
    of prison . . .
I want to call him – not Stalin – but Dzhugashvili!
I seem to see him dressed in his greatcoat and his cap,
On the wonderful square, with his *happy* eyes . . .
The furrows of his giant plough reach the sun.
He smiles with the smile of the harvester . . .

(from 'Lines on Stalin')   1937

You still haven't died, you're still not alone
While – with a beggar-woman for companion –
You delight in the immense plains
And the haze and cold and snow-storms.

In miraculous poverty, opulent privation,
You live alone – consoled, at peace;
These days and nights are hallowed,
Honey-tongued is this innocent labour.

Unhappy any man whom, like his shadow,
A dog's bark scares and the wind scythes down.
And poor indeed one who, half-alive,
Begs mercy of a shadow.

(354)   15–16 January 1937

I look the frost in the face, alone –
It's going nowhere, I come from nowhere –
And always the breathing wonder of the plain
Ironed, folded without a crease.

The sun is squinting in laundered destitution,
Its frown peaceful and consoled,
The multitude of forests much the same . . .
Snow crunches in my eyes, innocent as bread.

(349)   16 January 1937

Oh, these suffocating, asthmatic spaces of the steppes –
I'm sick of them! And the horizon,
Catching its breath, is flung wide-open.
I need a blindfold for both eyes!

I could better have endured the sand
In layers along the banks of the toothy Kama.
I would have clung to its shy sleeves,
Its ripples, brinks and hollows.

We would have worked in harmony – for a century or second.
Envious of the rapids' precipitation,
I would have listened under the flowing timber's bark
To the movement of the fibrous rings.

(351)   16 January 1937

9-10-57

Plagued by their miraculous and all-engulfing hunger,
What can we do with the murderous plains?
Surely what we deem to be their openness
We ourselves – falling asleep – behold;
And everywhere the questions swell – where do they go,
And where do they come from?
And is not he who makes us shriek in our sleep
Slowly crawling across them –
The space for Judases not yet born.

(350)   16 January 1937

Don't compare: anyone alive is matchless.
I yielded, with a kind of tender terror,
To the flatness of the plains,
And the circle of the sky made me ill.

I appealed to the air, my servant,
Waiting for service or news;
I prepared for a journey, swam along the arc
Of voyages that would never start.

I'm ready to wander where I shall have more sky.
But that bright longing cannot release me now
From the still-young hills of Voronezh
To the bright, all-human ones of Tuscany.

(352)   18 January 1937

What has contended with oxide and alloys
Burns like feminine silver,
And quiet work silvers the iron
Of the plough, the voice of the poet.

(353)   1937

The mounds of human heads disappear into the distance,
I dwindle there, no longer noticed,
But in caressing books, in children's games,
I shall rise from the dead to say: the sun!

(341)   1937

74

Listening, listening to the early ice
Rustling below the bridges,
I remember being luminously tipsy –
Head swimming, going under.

From callous stairways, areas of awkward palaces
On the edges of his Florence,
Alighieri sang more forcefully
From tired lips.

So too my shadow picks
At the grain of the granite,
Eyeing in the dark a row of hulks
That seemed houses in the light,

Or twiddles its thumbs
And yawns with us,
Or kicks up a row,
Warmed by other people's wine and sky,

And feeds stale loaves
To the importunate swans . . .

(358)   22 January 1937

A little boy, his red face shining like a lamp,
Lord and master of his sledge,
Careers across the steaming ice

And I – at odds with the obedient world – rejoice
In this contagion of toboggans,
Amazed by children swooping down:

Steep slopes, silver runners, frosty exhalations.
Oh that our era might slide for ever,
Soundless as squirrels, towards a soft river.

(from *359*)　*24 January 1937*

1-16-98

Where can I put myself this January?
Exposed, the town is extravagantly stubborn .
Have I got drunk on doors that lock me out? –
All the catches and fastenings make me want to bellow.

And yapping alleys stretched like stockings,
Streets tangled as an attic,
And cornered creatures crawling into corners
And scuttling out on the sly.

And I slither into a pit, into the warty dark,
Towards the iced-up pump-house,
And, stumbling, munch dead air,
And the feverish rooks rise up.

And I gasp after them, yelling
At some frozen wood-pile:
Just a reader, someone to speak with, a doctor!
A conversation on the bitter stairs!

(*360*)　*February 1937*

Like Rembrandt, martyr of light and dark,
I've gone into the depths of time –
And found it numb.
But one rib of mine is a burning spike
Which isn't guarded by these watching phantoms,
Nor by this sentry asleep under the storm.

Forgive me, magnificent brother, and master,
And father of the black-green darkness . . .
Like a boy following grown-ups into wrinkled water
I seem to be walking towards a future,
But it seems I shall never see it,
Now that our tribe is troubled by a shadow,
Twilight's intoxications, hollow years.

(from 265 and 364) Summer 1931 and 4 February 1937

Breaks of the rounded bays, shingle, blue,
And the slow sail continued as a cloud –
I'm parted from you, scarcely having known your worth.
Longer than organ fugues and bitter is the twisted seaweed,
Smelling of long-contracted falsities.
My head is tipsy with the tenderness of iron
And rust gnawing gently at the sloping shore . . .
Why does another sand lie under my head?
You – guttural Urals, muscular Volga,
These steppes – here are all my rights, –
And I must still inhale your air with my entire lungs.

(366)   4 February 1937

I sing when my throat is damp, my soul dry,
Sight fairly moist and the mind clear.
Are the grapes in good condition? The wine-skins?
And the stirrings of Colchis in the blood?
But my chest tightens, I'm tongue-tied:
It's no longer me singing – my breathing sings –,
My ears sheathed in mountains, head hollow.

An unmercenary song is its own reward:
Comfort for friends, for adversaries tar.

A single-eyed song, growing out of moss,
A single-voiced offering chanted on horses, on hills:
In quivering veins their blood is alive –
The hunters imbibe the wine, inhale the air,
Their only task a vexed and generous justice:
Single-mindedly to betroth and bring
The young pair, sinless, to their wedding.

(365)   8 February 1937

Eyes once keener than a sharpened scythe –
In the pupil a cuckoo, a drop of dew –

Now barely able to pick out, in full magnitude,
The lonely multitude of stars.

(368)   8–9 February 1937

Armed with the eyesight of narrow wasps
That suck at the axis of the earth,
I smell everything that's come my way,
Fruitlessly remembering it by heart.

I neither sing, nor draw,
Nor scrape a black-voiced bow across a string:
I only sting life, and love
To envy the energy of subtle wasps.

Oh if only heat of summer, sting of air,
Could – sidestepping sleep and death –
Some day goad me into hearing
The buzz of earth, buzz of the earth.

(367)   8 February 1937

I am plunged into a lion's den, a fort,
And sinking lower, lower, lower
Under the leavening shower of these sounds:
Stronger than lions, more potent than the Pentateuch.

How close the advent of your summons:
As keen as commandments of childbirth, of the first-born;
Like a string of pearls from Oceania
And meek baskets of Tahitian women.

Motherland of chastening songs, approach
With the deep notes of your resonant voice!
The shy-sweet countenance of wealthy daughters,
Primal mother, isn't worth your little finger.

My time is still unbounded.
And I have accompanied the rapture of the universe ✓
As muted organ pipes
Accompany a woman's voice.

(370)   12 February 1937

If our enemies take me
And people stop talking to me,
If they confiscate the whole world –
The right to breathe, open doors,
Affirm that existence shall go on
And that the people, like a judge, shall judge,
And if they dare to keep me like an animal
And fling my food on the floor,
I won't fall silent or deaden the agony,
But shall write what I am free to write,
My naked body gathering momentum like a bell,
And in a corner of the ominous dark
I shall yoke ten oxen to my voice
And move my hand in the darkness like a plough
And, wrung out into a legion of brotherly eyes,
Shall fall with the full heaviness of a harvest,
Exploding in the distance with all the force of a vow,   ✓
And in the depths of the unguarded night ✓
The eyes of that unskilled labourer, earth, shall shine
And a flock of flaming years swoop down,
And like a ripe thunderstorm Lenin shall burst forth.
But on this earth (which shall escape decay)
There to wake up life and reason will be – Stalin.

(372)   March 1937

Life's reticulations loosen, madness looms.
So a ray of light spun by a spider
Scatters ribbed pillars,
The crystal temples of eternity.

A thin beam of light to join them,
The columns of grateful pure lines
Shall gather intimately some time or other,
Like guests with an open countenance.

Only let it be now on earth, and not in heaven,
As in a house full of music. –
If only we don't scare or wound them –
It would be pleasant to survive.

Forgive me for what I'm telling you;
Quietly, quietly read it back to me.

(from *380*)   *15 March 1937*

This is what I want most of all:
With no one on my track
To soar behind the light
That I couldn't be farther from;

And for you to shine in that sphere –
There is no other happiness –
And learn from a star
What light could mean.

A star can only be star,
Light can only be light,
Because whispering warms us
And babbling makes us strong.

And I would like to say to you,
My little one, mumbling:
It's by means of our babbling
That I hand you to the light.

(384)   27 March 1937

This azure island was exalted by its potters –
Green Crete. In the resounding earth
They baked their gift. Do you hear the dolphin fins
Beat underground?

It's easy to remember the sea
In the clay enraptured by firing;
The cold power of a pot
Cleaves into sea and passion.

Azure island, volatile Crete,
Give me back what is mine – my labour;
From the breasts of the fruitful goddess
Fill the baked vessels.

This was, turned azure, and was sung,
Long before Ulysses,
Before food and drink
Were called 'my' and 'mine'.

Recover and shine again,
Star of ox-eyed heaven,
And fortuity, the flying fish,
And the sea saying *yes*.

(385)   March 1937

As if words were not enough,
The *theta* and *iota* of a Greek flute –
Unsculptural, unaccountable –
Matured, laboured, crossed frontiers.

It's impossible to forsake the flute:
It can't be stopped with clenched teeth,
It can't be prodded into speech with the tongue,
It can't be kneaded with the lips.

The flute player doesn't know repose –
It seems to him that he's alone,
That some time or other out of lilac clay
He formed his native sea.

With the urgency of recollecting lips,
With an ambitious, resonant murmur,
He collects the sounds to save them,
Neatly, stingily.

Later we shall not be able to repeat him,
Clods of clay in the sea's hands,
And when I am filled with the sea
My measure has become disease.

My own lips now lisp,
Plague or murder at the root.
And involuntarily falling, falling,
I diminish the force of the flute.

(387)   7 April 1937

I raise this greenness to my lips,
This sticky promise of leaves,
This breach-of-promise earth:
Mother of maples, of oaks, of snowdrops.

See how I am dazzled, blinded,
Obedient to the lowliest root.
Aren't they too much splendour for one's eyes –
The explosions of this park?

Like little balls of mercury, the frogs:
With their croaking they couple into a sphere;
Each twig becomes a branch,
And the air a chimera of milk.

(388)   30 April 1937

With her delightful uneven way of walking,
Limping on the empty earth,
A halting freedom draws her on.
It seems that a clear conjecture lingers in her gait –
Something to do with this Spring weather,
Original mother of the sepulchral dome.
And this shall always be beginning.

There are women who are natives of the sodden earth:
Their every step a hollow sobbing,
Their calling to accompany the risen,
To be first to meet the dead.
And we should trespass to demand caresses of them,
And to part from them is beyond our strength.

But whatever shall be is a promise only.

(from 394)   4 May 1937

Notes

In this rag-bag of notes I've set out to refer to and convey as wide a spectrum of information and bibliography as is succinctly possible. As the act of translation is necessarily an act of literary criticism, my own judgements, knowledge and ignorance are mainly embodied in my renderings.

Numbers are those of the Struve/Filippov edition, given after each poem. O.M. – Osip Mandelshtam; N. M. – Nadezhda Mandelshtam.

Where references to authors are unspecific, see under Acknowledgements (at the end of these Notes) for title and publisher.

STONE (1913, 1916, 1923 AND 1928)

Stone, the title of Mandelshtam's first book of poems, 'is obviously a prosaic symbol, yet timeless and in a way sacred – the material of which streets and cathedrals are made' (N. A. Nilsson, *Scando-Slavica* IX).

(14) 'The poem begins with a literally pregnant silence' (R. F. Holmes, private communication).

Peter France (*Poets of Modern Russia*): '"primordial speechlessness", the undifferentiated world which precedes poetry and human culture and whose image is the sea'.

V. Terras: 'O. M.'s nostalgia for primordial unity with the cosmos' (*Slavonic and East European Review* XVII, No. 109, 1969).

'He felt poetry to be immanent in nature, to *be* there in the silence, a presence with which he could be "fused" ... Poetry was not an occasion for sentiment, for "heart" ...' (Clarence Brown, *Mandelshtam*).

Robert Tracy has pointed out (in his *Osip Mandelshtam's 'Stone'*) that later, in O.M.'s *The one who walks*, 'he seems to reply to *Silentium*: "Though music cannot save one from the abyss"'.

Fyodor Tyutchev (1803–73) also wrote a celebrated poem called *Silentium*. (See Charles Tomlinson's *Versions from Fyodor Tyutchev*.)

(31) The poet Batyushkov (1787–1855) spent the last thirty or so years of his life in an asylum (from 1821). See also no. 261.

(32) R. F. Holmes has suggested to me that the 'age-old traveller' may be Pushkin.

(54) 'Joseph': Osip is a Russian version of Joseph.

(60) Ovid was banished to Scythia.

(80) Ovid is speaking.

TRISTIA (1922)

Tristia, the title of O.M.'s second book of poems, 'is a lament and an encomium for a splendid past, for Renaissance Venice, for Racine's France, for Hellas, above all for Petropolis . . . These cultures are seen as one, are fused into one . . . image of threatened civilisation . . . The theme of *Tristia* is summed up in a line of O.M.'s poem about Venice: "How can I escape this festive death?"' (Robert Chandler, from an unpublished article 'Mandelstam and Ezra Pound').

'In [O.M.'s] poems epochs and cultures that have become deeply stratified in language rise up before our consciousness. An individual word can summon them up . . .' (Boris Bukhshtab, *Russian Literature Triquarterly*, No. 1, 1971).

(82) Troezen was where Hippolytus died.

(89) Petropolis 'was Derzhavin's and Pushkin's name for Petersburg . . . A whole cultural tradition is threatened, dying'. 'It is not Athena, a goddess noted for her mercifulness and generosity, the goddess of wisdom, who reigns, but Proserpina, queen of the underworld' (S. Broyde).

(90) Dedicated to Marina Tsvetayeva. I have translated the poem in its original form, as given in Tsvetayeva's 'The history of one dedication' (*Oxford Slavonic Papers* XI, 1964).

(92) 'Tauris': the Crimea.

(93) 'the image of the "amulet buried in the sand" should be deciphered as "poetry addressed to the reader in posterity"' (K. Taranovsky).

'[O.M.'s] visions of classical antiquity are not "Homeric", "Sapphic", or "Horatian", but Mandelshtamian . . . It is "world culture", not ancient culture, that is the leitmotif of Mandelshtam's poetry' (Victor Terras, 'Classical Motifs in the Poetry of Osip Mandelshtam' (*Slavic and East European Journal*, 3, 1966).

Persephone (or Kore or Proserpina), Queen of the Underworld, spends two-thirds of the year with her mother Demeter (the Greek corn-goddess). 'This is the "light" part of the annual circle . . .' The black sail is 'still another topos of Greek mythology, known best from the myth of Theseus and Ariadne' (Victor Terras).

Line 20: 'Black rose-flakes' is an allusion to O.M.'s mother's death (see N.M., *Hope Abandoned*).

(104) Stanza 1: 'In the stillness of night a lover pronounces one tender name instead of another, and suddenly realises that this has happened once before: the words and the hair and the cock who has just crowed under the window crowed already in Ovid's *Tristia*. And he is overcome by a deep joy of recognition ...' (O.M., 'The Word and Culture', in *Sobraniye sochineniy*).

Line 4: 'M's elegy ... attains a genuine Latin ring, as Tynyanov observes, by introducing the entirely foreign word *vigilia*, which changes the chemistry of the whole stanza' (Henry Gifford, *Poetry in a Divided World*).

Stanza 3: Clarence Brown refers to 'the special kind of cognition that takes place when a poet composes a poem. Mandelshtam declares that this is in fact recognition' ('Mandelshtam's Notes Towards a Supreme Fiction', *Delos*, Austin, Texas, 1968, No. I).

Compare Fet's poem which begins: 'How threadbare our language!'

Line 25 onwards: see Pushkin, *Yevgeny Onegin* V: 4–10. 'The method [of divination] was to melt a candle into a shallow dish of water, where the suddenly cooled wax would assume odd shapes, like Rorschach blots or ... like a cloud or the stretched pelt of a squirrel ... Ovid's parting from his loved ones as he goes into exile is a paradigm of all partings' (Clarence Brown, *Mandelshtam*).

'Erebus': name of 'a place of darkness between Earth and Hades'. Erebus is the son of Chaos, brother of Night, and father of Day.

Joseph Brodsky's version of this poem can be inspected in his *Less than One*, Viking, 1986, p. 128.

(108) Line 4, according to Akhmatova, refers to the death of Pushkin; according to N.M., to the death of any human being. O.M.: 'Poetry is the plough which turns up *time*, so that the deepest layer of time – its black earth – appears on top.'

'The unspoken "name", the "golden care" of the second stanza is "love" ' (Leon Burnett, *The Modern Language Review*, April 1981).

(109) Written in the Crimea during the Civil War when O.M. and N.M. were not yet permanently together. 'Our relationship must have aroused in him a keen awareness of his Jewish roots, a tribal feeling, a sense of kinship with his people – I was the only Jewess in his life. He thought of the Jews as being one family, hence the theme of incest ... Leah was the name he had given to a daughter of Lot ... One night, thinking about me, he had suddenly seen that I would come to him, as Lot's daughters had to their father' (N.M., *Hope Abandoned*.)

(113) 'The word grows, bearing a green branch like the dove released from Noah's ark' (Lidija Ginzburg, 'The Poetics of Osip Mandelshtam', *Twentieth-Century Russian Literary Criticism*, edited by Victor Erlich, Yale University Press, 1975).

(116) Bees were sacred to Persephone, 'her messengers to Man' (N. A. Nilsson, *Mandelshtam: Five Poems*).

'The poetic word, metaphorically transformed into a kiss as a source of joy, is simultaneously a small, hairy bee which . . . has the orphic power of transmutation'; the necklace 'is a special artefact, composed of "dead bees", words which have perished in their normal usage; these "apian" words have reversed the normal process by converting honey into sunlight' (Tom Stableford, *The Literary Appreciation of Russian Writers*).

'The dense night forest of Taigetos': the high mountain overlooking Sparta, the domain of Artemis and Apollo, where the bees produce 'not the sweet honey of Hymettos but a honey with . . . a darker and wilder taste' (Nilsson).

(119) Line 16: See the *Odyssey*, Book IV, lines 219–84.

(124) Stanza 4: In a poem written in 1916, Mandelshtam alludes to Rome, Byzantium and Moscow – 'the three meetings of mankind and Providence . . . Byzantium had perished and the Grace of God had passed over to Russia' (K. Taranovsky).

Stanza 6: Henry Gifford (private communication): 'The slave who has overcome his fear is free – to endure unhappiness . . .'

POEMS (1928)

'Mandelshtam's *Poems* register a disintegration so absolute that the magnificent tragedy of *Tristia* is no longer possible, for tragedy presupposes the existence of generally accepted values' (Robert Chandler).

(127) Stanza 5 – 'conspirators': the Soviet edition substitutes 'dark people'.

(128) 'Tender Europa' is N.M.; the poem was written after their marriage.

(135) The question asked in the first stanza is answered in the second: the artist, the creator, can do these things.

O. Ronen refers to *Hamlet* as one of the subtexts:

> The time is out of joint; O cursed spite
> That ever I was born to set it right!

The original has four eight-line stanzas.

(136) 'this is an ode (Mandelshtam first subtitled it "a Pindaric fragment"), and, typically of the ode, it is concerned with itself, that is to say, with poetry. The world in which poetry must now exist is as turbulent as that of the forest and ship; everything cracks and shakes ... The principal image of the poem, the horseshoe itself, is what is left of the stormy animal, now dead ... This is human life frozen in its last attitudes, as though surprised in Herculaneum. The speaker himself now speaks in a resurrected voice, turned to stone, and time, the element that erupted ... at line 55, finally flows like lava over everything, obliterating the very self of the speaker at the end' (Clarence Brown, *Mandelshtam*.)

'A "poem" is uniquely able to remain intact while all else changes, and hence to contact an unknown future recipient of an expected gift in which is preserved also a part of the poet' (S. Broyde).

(140) 'A crucial "New Year". Lenin is mortally ill ...' (S. Monas, Notes to *Complete Poetry of Mandelshtam*). O. Ronen's *An Approach to Mandelshtam* includes a commentary on this poem: 'Clay': Ronen refers to Job ('Thou hast made me as the clay; and wilt thou bring me into dust again').

Three and half stanzas are untranslated.

Line 16: Ronen: 'but the singing lips of the age are sealed ...'

Line 21: Ronen: 'The theme of the forgotten or lost word of no. 113 ... is reinterpreted here and in other poems of 1921–25 (nos. 130, 131 and 136, etc.) in historical terms: the word becomes the heir-loom, passed from one generation to another, or lost in transmission.'

Line 35 – 'Fourth Estate': Ronen: '*not* the press, but the *raznochintsy* or classless intelligentsia (to which Mandelshtam felt that he belonged).'

Line 40 – 'the little bone of a pike': Ronen: 'Just as the horseshoe is, in *Whoever finds a horseshoe*, a talisman against hungry time, so the pike's bone ... becomes ... a talisman against ... the hungry State.'

Line 42 – 'Blissful laughter': 'the holiday laughter of the Saturnalia ...' etc.

Line 44 – 'the mighty sonatas': Ronen points to a passage from Mandelshtam's prose work *The Noise of Time* in which Herzen is mentioned, 'whose stormy political thought will always sound like a Beethoven sonata'.

(261) The original has six four-line stanzas.

(222) Lady Godiva: 'In 1040 Leofric, Earl of Mercia and Lord of Coventry, imposed certain exactions on his tenants, which his Lady besought him to remove. He said he would do so if she would ride naked through the town' (Brewer's *Dictionary of Phrase and Fable*).

(227) My version has benefited from Nabokov's salutary, scholastic savaging of Robert Lowell's adaptation of this poem (*New York Review of Books*, 4 December 1969).

(258) 'The paintings he most likely had in mind were Monet's *Lilas au soleil* and Pissarro's *Boulevard Montmartre* and *Place du Théâtre Français, Printemps*' (J. Baines).

(From 267 and 268) My abbreviated version combines two poems on Ariosto. 'The manuscripts and drafts [of the first] were taken away when we were searched in May 1934. In Voronezh, O.M. tried to remember the text, but his memory failed him and he wrote a second *Ariosto*. Soon, on a trip to Moscow, I found the 1933 *Ariosto* in one of my hiding-places. So there were now two poems with the same theme and material. This is a story in the spirit of the times – and I present it to future commentators' (N.M., from *Chapter 42*, translated by Donald Rayfield).

Line 2 – Peter the Great learnt how to shave beards, pull teeth and chop off heads. Through Peter, O.M. is alluding to Stalin.

(286) The poem that led to O.M.'s first arrest, in 1934. As he said to N.M.: 'Above all, I detest . . . fascism.'

Line 4 – 'man of the mountains': for this see the version by Richard and Elizabeth McKane in Osip Mandelshtam: The Moscow Notebooks (Bloodaxe, 1991).

From *Journey to Armenia*: Akhmatova wondered how, in 1933, this passage got past the censor. In fact, the editor of *Star*, a Leningrad literary journal, disobeyed the censor; it cost him his job, but he was not arrested.

Arshak – O.M.; Shapukh – Stalin; Darmastat – Bukharin (executed 1938), who was O.M.'s protector and responsible for his being able to journey to Armenia.

(296) Lament inspired by O.M.'s contemplation of N.M.'s fate. In 1934 O.M. was arrested and spent two weeks in the Lubianka prison, where he was interrogated and tortured. As a supreme and miraculous act of clemency on the part of the 'Boss', he was sentenced to only three years' exile; Stalin ordered that O.M. should be 'isolated but preserved'.

The rest of the poems in this book were composed in exile in Voronezh

Of the Voronezh poems D. Rayfield has said: 'The poet as a thinker, as an incarnation of the Hellenic spirit, barely functions. He is only an eye bewildered by forests, rivers, earth, wooden houses, the open spaces and the boundless sky of the steppes, which itself seems to him to be an eye on a cosmic plane. His thoughts are paralysed by an instinctive feeling of a predator's presence, the Kremlin which is now the axis on which the poet's world rotates' ('Mandelshtam's Voronezh poetry', *Russian Literature Triquarterly*, 1975); 'the poetry of 1933 and afterwards has a posthumous quality, breathing borrowed air on borrowed time' (*Grosseteste Review*; Vol. 7, Nos. 1–3. 'Deaths and Resurrections: the Later Poetry of Osip Mandelshtam').

(306) Curvature, like that of the earth's surface, is a curious feature of Red Square, both as viewed from one side to the other, and also along the other axis, as it slopes down to the River Moskva. 'Red Square symbolizes the rotten core of the system ... [The] Stalinist Terror ... knows no limits' (J. Baines).

(307) 'foot': 'the human and the metric foot which must both walk the black earth' (D. Rayfield).

'muttering lips': 'the symbol of [his] poetry' (J. Baines).

(318) N.M. brought O.M. 'a souvenir of the past, a small bag of stones from Koktebel ... [O.M.] affirms his predilection for the more prosaic pebbles from the sea' (J. Baines). There is an untranslatable pun in the second line: *opal* means 'opal', *opala* 'disgrace' in Russian.

(319) O.M. 'was beginning to see the soldiers as victims rather than oppressors, as vassals in the power of oriental-style despots, with their exotic retinues ... of janissaries and eunuchs' (J. Baines).

'Lines on Stalin': O.M.'s 'positive' ode to Stalin. The original consists of seven twelve-line stanzas.

In January 1937, in exile, with the rope around his neck, O.M. tried to write an ode in praise of Stalin to save his wife's life and his own. The attempt failed: this is part of the remarkably ambiguous result.

See *Slavic Review*, 1975; Bengt Jangfeldt: 'O.M.'s "Ode" to Stalin', *Scando-Slavica*, 1976; Clarence Brown: 'Into the Heart of Darkness: Mandelshtam's Ode to Stalin', *Slavic Review*, 1967; and J. Baines: *Mandelshtam: The Later Poetry*.

(350) 'The historical perspective which caused Mandelshtam to see [Stalin] as the Judas not so much of present but of future generations was

seldom achieved by his contemporaries in 1937, at the height of the Terror' (J. Baines).

(354) Third stanza, line 4: the 'shadow' Mandelshtam might have 'begged favour of' is Stalin.

(358) Henry Gifford (in a letter to me): 'The "stale loaves" suggest to me Dante's bread that tastes of salt, or what is called in *Richard II* "the bitter bread of banishment".'

(366) 'Urals': in 1934 Mandelshtam was exiled to the Urals, to Cherdyn (where – thinking he was going to be arrested again by the secret police – he threw himself out of the window of the hospital), and travelled along the Volga to arrive there.

'These steppes' refers to the area around Voronezh.

I am indebted to R. Chandler for drawing my attention to the fact that 'here are all my rights' refers to Pushkin's poem *From Pindemonte* (1836), in which he says he doesn't mind about censorship, not having the right to vote, etc.; all he cares about is that he should be left to himself, not have to give account to others of what he does, and be free to wonder at the godlike beauties of nature and art: 'Here is my happiness! Here are my rights . . .'

R. F. Holmes has pointed out to me that 'of course both poets *did* care about other things than being left to themselves . . . Mandelshtam, besides attacking Stalin, attacked one Caesar at least, two Tsars, Napoleon, Hitler and Mussolini.' (In *Rome*, composed in 1937, Rome is characterized as a 'nursery for murder'; 'The degenerate chin of the dictator/Sags over Rome').

(367) This poem was written during the time when Mandelshtam was particularly obsessed with Joseph Stalin. Wasp, in Russian, is *osa*, axis is *os'*. Joseph, in Russian, can be either *Osip* or *Iosif*.

O.M. 'obviously listed here some of the arts officially . . . encouraged in the mid-thirties, the period of violin-competitions, portrait-painting, the revival of the classical opera . . .' (O. Ronen, *An Approach to Mandelshtam*).

(368) The last poem in Mandelshtam's Stalin cycle. Scythe, in Russian, is 'kosa'. The cuckoo, as also in 'the cuckoo is weeping in its stone tower' (no. 121), alludes to a passage from *The Lay of Igor's Campaign*, a twelfth-century poem in which Yaroslavna, Igor's wife, mourns him 'like a desolate cuckoo'. 'On the Danube Yaroslavna's voice is heard: like a desolate cuckoo she cries early in the morning. "I will fly," she says, "like a cuckoo along the Danube, I will dip my sleeve of beaver-

fur in the river Kayala, I will wipe the Prince's bleeding wounds . . ."' (*Penguin Book of Russian Verse*, edited by D. Obolensky). '[Mandelshtam] lamented his failing eyesight, which had once been "sharper than a whetted scythe" but had not had time to pick out each of the "lonely multitude of stars".' (N.M., *Hope Against Hope*.)

(370) Here O.M., according to D. Rayfield, sees himself as Daniel who championed Israel (*Russian Literature Triquarterly*, 1975).

'The singer is free to descend into the lion's den, since her voice can conquer the lion, escape from the fortress – Marian Anderson's speciality was negro spirituals . . .' (J. Baines).

The poem combines two images: of Marian Anderson, whose deep voice O.M. had heard on the radio; and of a singer friend whose husband had just been re-arrested after recent release from five years in a camp. (See *Hope Against Hope*, chapter 39.)

(384) N.M., the 'child' or 'little one', is entrusted in this lullaby to the care of the stars because 'the radiance of the stars is also that of his poetry' (J. Baines).

O.M. was embarrassed, as far as eventual publication might be concerned, by the intimacy of what he called 'these verses of the bed'.

(385) '. . . Hera was first worshipped in the form of a cow' (J. Baines).

(387) 'The Greek flute's sounds are clearly the poetic force before it has been precipitated in language . . . [The] flute's music . . . crosses barriers, it is unselfconscious . . . The poet creates his own past; "making his native sea" out of clay, like the Cretan potters . . . [But] the flautist is in the past, unrepeatable. He is what the poet might have been or continued being, had the Hellenic world not fallen apart. Now nothing works: the sea gives no birth . . . [it] kills instead of giving life . . . [Mandelshtam's] lips cannot work the flute, and the balance of forces . . . topples, leaving only the destructive, negative force to silence poetry . . . If there is a moral in the poem, it is that the poet, conscious of his individual death, is tainted by his fear and loses his gift of immersing himself in the medium of poetry' (D. Rayfield, *Russian Literature Triquarterly*, 1975).

Rayfield points out that *sea* (*more*) changes into its phonetic twin *plague* (*mor*) – which I have rendered as *disease*; similarly the 'syllable *ub* joins the flautist's mouth (*zuby*, teeth, and *guby*, lips) in a fatal conjunction with death (*ub*iystvo, murder . . .). – This sort of thing, of course, drives the translator to despair, if not self-destruction.

N.M. writes about this poem in *Hope Against Hope*, chapter 39: 'Since he works with his voice, a poet's lips are the tools of his trade,

and in . . . [this] poem O.M. is also speaking about his own whispering
lips and the painful process of converting into words the sounds
ringing in his ears . . . The poem is . . . about a flute player we knew
. . . He would bring great comfort to O.M. by playing Bach or
Schubert for him. Schwab . . . [was] accused of espionage and sent to
a camp for common criminals . . . He was already an old man and he
ended his days there.'

(388) Henry Gifford discusses an early poem by Pasternak where the latter
mentions 'sticky greenery', which seems to evoke the 'sticky little
leaves opening in spring' that reconciled Ivan Karamazov to life
(Henry Gifford, *Pasternak*).

(394) The limping woman was Natasha Shtempel, whom the Mandelshtams
knew in Voronezh.

ACKNOWLEDGEMENTS

Passages from the following works are quoted in the Notes by permission:

Jennifer Baines, *Mandelshtam: The Later Poetry* (Cambridge University Press,
1976).

Clarence Brown, *Mandelshtam* (Cambridge University Press, London and
New York, 1973).

Steven Broyde, *Osip Mandelshtam and His Age* (Harvard University Press,
1975).

Peter France, *Poets of Modern Russia* (Cambridge University Press, 1982).

Henry Gifford, *Pasternak* (Cambridge University Press, 1977).

Poetry in a Divided World (Cambridge University Press, 1986).

Nadezhda Mandelshtam, *Hope Against Hope* and *Hope Abandoned*, copyright
© 1970 and copyright © 1972 respectively by Atheneum Publishers;
English translation copyright © 1970 and copyright © 1973, 1974
respectively by Atheneum Publishers, New York and Harvill Press
Ltd, London (published by Atheneum Publishers, New York, and
William Collins and Harvill Press, London).

Chapter 42 and Osip Mandelshtam, *'The Goldfinch' and Other Poems*, trans-
lated with an introduction by Donald Rayfield (The Menard Press,
1973).

Osip Mandelshtam, *Complete Critical Prose and Letters*, edited by Jane Gary
Harris, translated by Jane Gary Harris and Constance Link (Ardis,
1979).

·

Osip Mandelshtam: Selected Essays, translated and edited with an introduction by Sidney Monas (University of Texas Press, 1977).

Osip Mandelshtam's 'Stone', translated with an introduction by Robert Tracy (Princeton University Press, 1981).

Sidney Monas, notes to *Complete Poetry of Osip Mandelshtam*, translated by Burton Raffel and Alla Burago (by permission of the State University of New York Press; copyright © 1973 State University of New York).

N. A. Nilsson, *Osip Mandelshtam: Five Poems* (Almqvist & Wiksell International, Stockholm, 1974).

The Penguin Book of Russian Verse, introduced and edited by Dimitri Obolensky, copyright © Dimitri Obolensky, 1962, 1963 (Penguin Books, 1962, rev. ed. 1965).

Omry Ronen, *An Approach to Mandelshtam* (The Magnes Press, The Hebrew University, Jerusalem, 1983).

Tom Stableford, *The Literary Appreciation of Russian Writers* (Cambridge University Press, 1981).

Kiril Taranovsky, *Essays on Mandelshtam* (Harvard University Press, 1976).

Further Reading: a Select Bibliography

BOOKS

Baines, Jennifer, *Mandelshtam: The Later Poetry*, Cambridge University Press, 1976.

Blot, Jean, *Osip Mandelshtam*, Poètes d'aujourd'hui 206, Seghers, Paris, 1972.

Broyde, S., *Osip Mandelshtam and His Age: War and Revolution in the Poetry 1913–1923*, Harvard Slavic Monographs 1, 1975.

Brown, Clarence (translation), *The Prose of Osip Mandelshtam*, North Point Press, Berkeley, CA; Quartet, London, 1967.

Mandelshtam, Cambridge University Press, 1973.

Cohen, Arthur A., *O. E. Mandelshtam: An Essay in Antiphon*, Ardis, Ann Arbor, Michigan, 1974.

Freidin, Grigory, *A Coat of Many Colours*, Berkeley, CA, 1988.

Isenberg, Charles, *Substantial Proofs of Being: Osip Mandelshtam's Literary Prose*, Slavica, Ohio, 1987.

Harris, Jane Gary (translation and introduction), *Mandelshtam: The Complete Critical Prose and Letters*, Ardis, Ann Arbor, Michigan, 1979.

Osip Mandelshtam, Twayne, Boston, 1988.

Koubourlis, Dimitri, *A Concordance to the Poems of Osip Mandelshtam*, Cornell University Press, Ithaca and London, 1974.

Mandelstam, Nadezhda Yakovlevna, *Hope Against Hope*, Atheneum, New York and Collins and Harvill, London, 1976.

Hope Abandoned, Atheneum, New York and Collins and Harvill, London 1973.

Mozart and Salieri. An Essay on Osip Mandelshtam and Poetic Creativity, Ardis, Ann Arbor, Michigan, 1973.

Monas, Sidney (translation and introduction), *Osip Mandelshtam: Selected Essays*, University of Texas, Austin, 1977.

Nilsson, Nils Åke, *Osip Mandelshtam: Five Poems*, Uppsala, 1974.

Przybylski, Ryszard, *An Essay on the Poetry of Osip Mandelshtam: God's Grateful Guest*. Ardis, Ann Arbor, Michigan, 1987.

Rayfield, Donald (introduction and translations), Nadezhda Mandelshtam, *Chapter 42*, and Osip Mandelshtam, '*The Goldfinch*' *and Other Poems*, The Menard Press, London, 1973.

Ronen, Omry, *An Approach to Mandelshtam*, The Magnes Press, Jerusalem, 1983.

Struve, Nikita, *Osip Mandelshtam*, Institut d'Études Slaves, Paris, 1982.

Taranovsky, Kiril, *Essays on Mandelshtam*, Harvard University Press, Cambridge, Mass. and London, 1976.

Tracy, Robert (translation and introduction), *Osip Mandelshtam's 'Stone'*, Princeton University Press, N.J. and Guildford, Surrey, 1981.

West, Daphne M., *Mandelshtam: The Egyptian Stamp*, Birmingham Slavonic Monographs No. 10, University of Birmingham, 1980.

Zeeman, Peter, *The Later Poetry of Osip Mandelshtam: Text and Context*, Rodopi, Amsterdam, 1988.

ARTICLES

Bodin, Per-Arne, 'Understanding the Sign: an Analysis of 'Sredi svyashchennikov . . .', *Scando-Slavica*, Stockholm, 31, 1985, pp. 31–9.

Brown, Clarence, 'Into the Heart of Darkness: Mandelshtam's Ode to Stalin', *Slavic Review*, Stanford, CA, December 1967, pp. 584–604.

'Mandelshtam's Notes towards a Supreme Fiction', *Delos*, Austin, Texas, 1968, pp. 32–48.

Brown, Clarence and Hughes, Robert (translators), 'Mandelshtam: Talking about Dante', *Delos*, 6, 1971.

Freidin, Grigory, 'The Whisper of History and the Noise of Time in the Writings of Osip Mandelshtam', *Russian Review*, XXXVII/4 Columbus, OH, October 1978, pp. 421–37.

Harris, Jane Gary, 'The "Latin Gerundive" as Autobiographical Imperative: a Reading of Mandelshtam's Journey to Armenia', *Slavic Review*, 45, 1986, pp. 1–19.

Monas, Sidney (translation and introduction), *Osip Mandelshtam: Journey to Armenia*, George F. Ritchie, San Francisco, 1979.

Nilsson, Nils Åke, 'Osip Mandelshtam and His Poetry', *Scando-Slavica*, 4, 1963, pp. 37–59.

'To Kassandra: a Poem by Osip Mandelshtam', *Poetica Slavica*, Ottawa, 1981, pp. 39–49.

Rayfield, Donald, 'The Flight from Chaos', *European Judaism*, Amsterdam, 1971–2, pp. 37–41.

'A Winter in Moscow (Osip Mandelshtam's poems of 1933–34)', *Stand*, Newcastle upon Tyne, XIV/1, 1972, pp. 18–23.

'Deaths and Resurrections', *Grosseteste Review*, Lincoln, 7/1–3, 1974, pp. 156–77.

'Mandelshtam: the Voronezh Notebooks', *Russian Literature Triquarterly*, Ann Arbor, Michigan, 11, 1975, pp. 323–62.

'Lamarck and Mandelshtam', *Scottish Slavonic Review*, Glasgow, 9, autumn 1987, pp. 85–101.

Struve, Nikita, 'Les Thèmes chrétiens dans l'oeuvre d'Osip Mandelshtam', *Essays in Honor of George Florovsky*, II: *The Religious World of Russian Culture. Russia and Orthodoxy*, Mouton, Amsterdam, 1975, pp. 305–13.

Terras, Victor, 'Classical Motifs in the Poetry of Osip Mandelshtam', *Slavic and East European Journal*, Quebec, X/3, 1966, pp. 251–67.

'The Time Philosophy of Mandelshtam', *Slavonic and East European Review*, London, XLVII, 1969, pp. 344–54.

Vitins, Ieva, 'Mandelshtam's Farewell to Marina Tsvetaeva', *Slavic Review*, XLVI/2, 1987, pp. 266–80.

Zeeman, Peter, 'Reference and Interpretation (Mandelshtam)', *Russian Literature*, Amsterdam, XVIII, 1985, pp. 256–98.

'Irony in Mandelshtam's Later Poetry', *Russian Literature*, XIX, 1986, pp. 405–44.

'Metaphorical Language in Mandelshtam', *Russian Literature*, XXI, 1987, pp. 313–46.

READ MORE IN PENGUIN

In every corner of the world, on every subject under the sun, Penguin represents quality and variety – the very best in publishing today.

For complete information about books available from Penguin – including Puffins, Penguin Classics and Arkana – and how to order them, write to us at the appropriate address below. Please note that for copyright reasons the selection of books varies from country to country.

In the United Kingdom: Please write to *Dept. EP, Penguin Books Ltd, Bath Road, Harmondsworth, West Drayton, Middlesex UB7 ODA*

In the United States: Please write to *Consumer Sales, Penguin USA, P.O. Box 999, Dept. 17109, Bergenfield, New Jersey 07621-0120*. VISA and MasterCard holders call 1-800-253-6476 to order Penguin titles

In Canada: Please write to *Penguin Books Canada Ltd, 10 Alcorn Avenue, Suite 300, Toronto, Ontario M4V 3B2*

In Australia: Please write to *Penguin Books Australia Ltd, P.O. Box 257, Ringwood, Victoria 3134*

In New Zealand: Please write to *Penguin Books (NZ) Ltd, Private Bag 102902, North Shore Mail Centre, Auckland 10*

In India: Please write to *Penguin Books India Pvt Ltd, 706 Eros Apartments, 56 Nehru Place, New Delhi 110 019*

In the Netherlands: Please write to *Penguin Books Netherlands bv, Postbus 3507, NL-1001 AH Amsterdam*

In Germany: Please write to *Penguin Books Deutschland GmbH, Metzlerstrasse 26, 60594 Frankfurt am Main*

In Spain: Please write to *Penguin Books S. A., Bravo Murillo 19, 1° B, 28015 Madrid*

In Italy: Please write to *Penguin Italia s.r.l., Via Felice Casati 20, I–20124 Milano*

In France: Please write to *Penguin France S. A., 17 rue Lejeune, F–31000 Toulouse*

In Japan: Please write to *Penguin Books Japan, Ishikiribashi Building, 2–5–4, Suido, Bunkyo-ku, Tokyo 112*

In Greece: Please write to *Penguin Hellas Ltd, Dimocritou 3, GR–106 71 Athens*

In South Africa: Please write to *Longman Penguin Southern Africa (Pty) Ltd, Private Bag X08, Bertsham 2013*

READ MORE IN PENGUIN

INTERNATIONAL POETS – A SELECTION

Octavio Paz Selected Poems
Winner of the 1990 Nobel Prize for Literature

'His poetry allows us to glimpse a different and future place ... liberating and affirming' – James Wood in the *Guardian*

Fernando Pessoa Selected Poems

'I have sought for his shade in those Edwardian cafés in Lisbon which he haunted, for he was Lisbon's Cavafy or Verlaine' – Cyril Connolly in the *Sunday Times*

Yehuda Amichai Selected Poems
Translated by Chana Bloch and Stephen Mitchell

'A truly major poet ... there's a depth, breadth and weighty momentum in these subtle and delicate poems of his' – Ted Hughes

Czesław Miłosz Collected Poems 1931–1987
Winner of the 1980 Nobel Prize for Literature

'One of the greatest poets of our time, perhaps the greatest' – Joseph Brodsky

Joseph Brodsky To Urania
Winner of the 1987 Nobel Prize for Literature

Exiled from the Soviet Union in 1972, Joseph Brodsky has been universally acclaimed as the most talented Russian poet of his generation.

and

Paul Celan	Selected Poems
Tony Harrison	Selected Poems *and* Theatre Works 1973–1985
Heine	Selected Verse
Geoffrey Hill	Collected Poems
Philippe Jaccottet	Selected Poems
Osip Mandelstam	Selected Poems
Peter Redgrove	Poems 1954–1987